Law Firm Innovation: Insights and Practice

EDITED BY LAURA SLATER

Contents

Executive summary

THE LEGAL services market is evolving at pace, driven by new technologies and a greater variety of service providers, and perhaps even more so, by clients who are more demanding, discerning, and selective than ever before about the way their legal services are delivered. In addition to all of this, a new generation of lawyers with very different attitudes and ambitions to those that went before them are emerging in the legal marketplace with different expectations about how they want to work and the type of organisation they want to be a part of. Innovation is springing up not just from new arrivals shaking up the market, but increasingly within in-house legal teams who are finding novel ways to stretch tightening resources to balance a growing workload, and from traditional law firms who are feeling the pressure to differentiate.

None of this should be news to law firm leaders, however, and 'innovation' is a word that is undoubtedly used more than ever in the legal market. But what is innovation in a law firm context? In what ways can an undeniably traditional industry demonstrate innovation, and how do individual law firms show what innovation means to them? *Law Firm Innovation: Insights and Practice* not only answers these questions, but it also provides an overview of innovation options and practices in a changing legal marketplace. It offers practical advice for firms that are looking to become more innovative in the way they work, and it provides first-hand examples of innovation within the legal industry from around the globe.

The book is divided into two parts. In the first section, a series of articles from experts and practitioners explore the way the market is changing and provide practical guidance and frameworks designed to help law firms and departments to introduce innovation as a core business activity. In the second part of the book, case studies from some of the most innovative legal service providers allow the reader to explore some of the ground-breaking approaches already being taken by their peers, and to potentially benchmark their firm and innovation abilities against what is already being demonstrated as innovation in the market.

Part one opens with an overview of disruptive innovation in the legal service industry, based on the authors' in-depth research in this area. The authors find that, while new market entrants do in some cases have the potential to replace at least parts of the traditional law firm service offering – a threat to 'traditional' providers that is only going to increase – it is the companies who foot the bill for both 'traditional' and 'alternative' providers who will ultimately be responsible for driving the future of innovation in the legal industry.

Whether working in-house, at a legacy firm, or as part of an alternative provider, as one contributor to this report remarks: 'Innovative people will always have good ideas. The real challenge… is to cultivate innovation better'. This key challenge is the subject of the second and third chapters. One chapter describes the foundations on which a firm can build a more systematic and intentional approach to innovation, the barriers firms are likely to encounter, and how these may be overcome. The second looks more specifically at how knowledge management – which in most law firms is geared towards improving access to knowledge or expertise – can instead be leveraged to create a culture where innovation is part of the fabric of the firm.

The article that follows this then introduces several powerful frameworks of strategic innovation and explains how they can be mixed and matched in a variety of unique combinations in order to suit an individual organisation.

Part one then concludes with a discussion of pricing innovation, and, in the final chapter, an exploration of the next logical step for law firms: technology that will allow firms to easily track the profitability of these new pricing structures, and to track client and matter fees more generally. The report continues with specific case study examples of law firm innovation in Part two.

Innovation within any organisation cannot exist without employee engagement, and one firm that has understood this remarkably well is Baker & McKenzie. The first of the case studies in Part two describes Baker & McKenzie's approach to personnel management, the current initiatives that have seen the global firm widely recognised as one of the world's most innovative law firms, and the steps it is taking to ensure that its people continue to define and drive its culture and working practices.

For employees to feel truly engaged with a business, their values must be aligned with those of the organisation so that they derive meaning from their work – so says the managing partner of Marque Lawyers. In the second of the case studies, the MP of the Sydney-based firm candidly talks about the pressures in the legal marketplace, the values that drive Marque Lawyers and set it apart, and explains why it's an exciting time to be a lawyer – for those who can see past the threats to the opportunities of an overcrowded market.

Another legal services provider that places a high value on well-rounded, engaged employees is AdventBalance, which, since contributing to ARK Group's first innovation report in 2011 (in its previous incarnation as AdventLawyers), has gone on to become the fastest-growing alternative provider of legal services in the Asia Pacific. In an in-depth interview, the company's managing director for Asia, John Knox, contrasts the Asian and Australian market with the US and UK in terms of appetite for innovation, and he provides in-depth advice on why an innovative and alternative model such as theirs offers a win-win for firm and client.

Another firm with a truly client-centric approach is gunnercooke. A case study from the senior-lawyer-only firm explains why its pioneering approach, combining quality assurance and a more flexible, transparent approach of a young firm is so attractive to commercial clients.

Finally, Part two concludes with an insight into Riverview Law from the company's chairman, Karl Chapman, who talks about the features of the legal market that make it unique with respect to other industries, why legislative changes have made the UK a great place to embrace technology-led legal services, and the dangers of failing to move with the times.

With 'appetite for new service delivery models' increasing,[1] change and innovation is not something law firms can shy away from. It is clear that the market is changing, and that those that fail to move with the times will be left behind. This report highlights some of the approaches that can be taken – and many that are already being successfully employed – by law firms of various sizes. In using the guidance in this report, law firm leaders can discover how to build a true culture of innovation and work towards creating a more agile, inclusive, and prepared firm to meet and respond to the unexpected challenges and opportunities of a future where innovation will no longer be optional.

Reference

1. According to Allen & Overy's 2014 Law Firm Survey. For the full survey, see: www.allenovery.com/SiteCollectionDocuments/global-survey-lsm.pdf.

PART ONE

Strategies and tactics for innovation

Chapter 1: Disruptive innovation

By Markus Hartung, director, and Arne Gärtner, research assistant, at the Bucerius Center on the Legal Profession (CLP) at Bucerius Law School, Hamburg

'CONSULTING ON the cusp of disruption' is the title of a widely recognised article about the future of the consulting industry that was published in the October 2013 issue of the *Harvard Business Review*. The Harvard academics who penned the article (among them the undisputed expert in the field of disruptive innovation, Clayton M. Christensen[1]) predicted serious changes – disruption – for the consulting industry. Backing up this prediction, they held up law firms as proof that not even professional services firms are guarded against radical change. Citing many trends that are widely known in the legal industry – the disaggregation of the value chain of traditional law firms, greater use of contract attorneys, the development of new business models and the rise of alternative service providers, and a generally eroding opacity of the law firm business model – the authors plainly showed that, in their eyes, the legal industry was already far from 'the cusp of disruption'. It was already in the middle of radical change.

The image of the legal industry as a pioneer in the field of disruptive innovation surprised us, since the industry (and especially lawyers) are usually perceived as being rather conservative, and law firms are usually regarded as being the late majority (or even the laggards) when it comes to their rate of adaption to innovation and change. Thinking about this image, we were curious if – on the grounds of our ongoing research on trends in the legal industry – we would find any evidence to prove the thesis presented in the article.

Firstly, we came to the conclusion that our research in the past had focused too much on traditional law firms, legal departments, and their mutual relationship, and not enough on new business models, new services, and alternative providers. The theory of disruptive innovation, however, is based on the belief that new market entrants drive disruptive innovation. Thus, the idea for a new study was born.

Together with The Boston Consulting Group, in 2014, we carried out a fundamental study on the future of the legal industry. In the course of the study, titled 'Trends in the legal market – disruption, evolution or just hype?', more than 60 interviews and workshops with legal departments, alternative providers, law firms, and other market experts were carried out. In addition, we conducted an extensive literature review on the overarching topics of strategy, innovation, trends, and the future of the legal market. The main target of the study was to analyse the direction in which the legal market is now headed, and to establish who is in the driver's seat for market developments in the long-run.

Innovation in the legal market

Before we discuss the details and findings of the study, a brief overview of innovation in the legal market might be helpful for a general understanding of the term 'innovation' in this context. 'Innovation' means everything that is new and, at the same time, has an economic potential. Being creative and coming up with something new is not sufficient for something to be called 'innovative'. A lot of what lawyers are doing is highly creative in terms of finding unique solutions to unique problems, but it is not innovative, since these ideas cannot be packaged as 'legal products', sold to other clients, or protected under patent or copyright laws. Even if lawyers come up with radically new ideas or products, they cannot protect their ideas.

Every innovation can be categorised in terms of several different dimensions. One dimension is the type of innovation: distinguishing between innovative products, services, processes, or business models. Intensity of innovation is another dimension that makes it possible to distinguish between different kinds of innovation: sustaining, radical, or disruptive.

To lawyers, innovation may sound like something strange and new at first. The pre-crisis legal market was characterised by excess demand. This, combined with two of the main characteristics of the law firm business model (opacity of the delivery model and information asymmetry), made lawyers guarded against innovation and change. Therefore, lawyers didn't need to think about innovation for a long time, and due to the surplus in demand, clients were not in the position to drive innovation and change. That's why lawyers, who are confronted with innovation, especially those from big law firms, usually focus on the question: 'why should law firms or legal departments be innovative at all?' As a consequence, they often come up with a number of arguments as to why lawyers and law firms *don't* need to be innovative. But that is the wrong question to ask. The right question is: 'why not?'

What makes lawyers so special that they don't need to innovate? Every business in the world needs to innovate in order to gain competitive advantage and survive in the marketplace – and lawyers are no longer an exception to this basic rule. But the fact that lawyers today need to be innovative doesn't necessarily create an environment that automatically leads to disruptive innovation. Hence, in the course of the study, we were looking for the 'conditio sine qua non' of disruptive innovation.

Where does disruption come from?

The theory of disruptive innovation suggests that there are usually new business models or products that disrupt whole markets and, in the end, cast out other (including the leading) market participants – traditional law firms, in our case. That is why we started to analyse different business models and services of various alternative service providers. Further, we examined the value chain and business model of big law firms regarding the question of which elements of the business model alternative providers try to attack and whether this implies any disruptive potential. Finally, we analysed the adoption rate of new services and business models from the in-house perspective in order to analyse the market penetration of alternative providers. We realised that we had underestimated the role of alternative services providers and that they definitely need to be considered when discussing or analysing the future of the legal industry. We therefore came to the conclusion that we are on the verge of a new legal ecosystem, which now has three groups of market participants.

Alternative providers: A broad range of different firms

Today, alternative service providers are broadly described as market participants with a non-traditional (including non-lawyer) business models. This definition is imprecise, almost meaningless. What is 'traditional' in this regard? The traditional law firm business model is normally referred to as a partnership with the classical pyramid model and a leverage structure. Non-traditional or alternative (as in an alternative to the traditional law firm) providers, on the other hand, are often organised as corporations, rather than partnerships, and are oriented around fundamentally different rules and goals. There are alternative business models that have existed for a long time now, but equally there are new business models that have only been developed in recent years.

Our research found, accordingly, that the lack of a distinction between categories of alternative service provider made it impossible to form a general statement as to whether they might disrupt the legal industry. The business models and innovative ideas of the various alternative providers are simply too fundamentally different. That is why our study – for the first time – classified alternative service providers into different categories, based on their business models and the services they offer. We found a total of eight different types of alternative providers.

Classification of alternative providers

The longest-established and best-known alternative providers are insourcing/lawyers on demand firms and legal process outsourcing (LPO) firms that mostly deliver standardised and partly automated tasks in the fields of due diligence or e-discovery. These are the most successful models in terms of market penetration and size of firm. In addition to LPO and insourcing firms, we identified six other types of alternative providers. There are a number of providers already active in all of these areas. The categories can be described as follows:

1. **Legal process outsourcing** (LPO) firms provide low-cost work with low complexity/criticality. Firms include Pangea3, Axiom, or CPA Global.
2. **Insourcing** firms offer temporary legal staffing services to cover peaks or gaps at legal departments and law firms. Examples are Axiom, Lawyers On Demand, or Eversheds Agile.
3. **Providers of complex projects/managed legal services** include, on the one hand, big management consultant and audit firms like BCG, McKinsey, PwC, EY, or Deloitte, and on the other hand firms like Axiom, Radiant Law, or Riverview Law. They provide services for the management of more complex/critical projects, often with extended responsibilities.
4. **Alternative/virtual law firms** provide traditional legal advice services, but without the typical overhead costs and often on a fixed-fee basis. The lawyers are virtually connected. Virtual law firms include Clearspire (which was still going at the time of the study) and gunnercooke.
5. **Self-service platforms** are tailored platforms for legal needs and questions. They offer both legal document generation services, as well as supplementary legal advice and Q&A. Online resolution platforms are self-service platforms as well. Examples are Legal Zoom, Modria, or Rocket Lawyer.
6. **Providers of research and information services** offer customised legal research on demand. Their research is based on databases and libraries. Firms offering research and information services include Thomson Reuters and Lois Law.
7. **Quantitative legal analytics** providers offer high-end statistical products, for instance statistics to predict law suit outcomes or IT-based management of billings. Examples are TyMetrics, Lawyer Metrics, and Lex Machina.
8. **Networking platforms** are structured to enable the exchange of legal information, e.g. collaboration systems for in-house counsel in the form of closed communities. See for example Legal OnRamp or Advance Law.

All of the firms listed above have entered the marketplace with innovative ideas and business models. But it is still an open question whether these firms have the potential to disrupt the legal industry. To answer this question, it is important to analyse each firm's 'point of attack'.

Point of attack: The value chain of law firms

Alternative business models try to exploit at least one shortcoming of traditional law firms. Three of the most common weaknesses of law firms are (i) lack of sufficient IT – in terms of collaboration and knowledge management systems, (ii) lack of project management skills – in terms of management of complex projects where legal is only one part of a bigger picture, and (iii) lack of efficiency – in terms of high costs and poor processes. Therefore, the business models of alternative providers are usually IT-driven, efficiency-driven, or project management-driven. Some of the providers strive in more than one direction.

But the value chain of traditional law firms can be further differentiated between primary and secondary or support activities. Although there is no common or unanimous view on primary and secondary activities, we would argue that primary activities are in general resources planning, project management, information gathering, legal research, negotiation, and contract drafting. Secondary activities are supportive of law firm infrastructure, human resources management, procurement, business development, innovation, and strategy.

Regarding primary activities, most of the above-described models only offer services that change a part of the value chain of traditional law firms. Lawyers On Demand, for example, aim to offer better options for resources planning, but no legal services. Or consider LPO: they deal with simple, and often standardised, tasks – e.g. electronic discovery, information gathering, due diligence services – but they don't offer legal advice. And then there are firms that offer legal information and research services, aiming to offer better value for money to law firms and legal departments. Thus, six of these categories mainly offer specialised, niche products and don't really compete with traditional law firms. They offer services that might replace parts of the value chain of law firms, but they cannot replace law firms entirely. That doesn't mean that these firms cannot be profitable; on the contrary, the specialisation might lead to a very good market position with good margins. Firms specialising in only a small part of the value chain can be very successful, but we assume that they cannot foster radical change and disruption. Only virtual law firms and providers of managed legal services, partly offering the same services as traditional law firms, try to supersede traditional law firms in large part, and thus might carry the potential to replace some services law firms are offering.

At the present time, alternative providers are mainly focused on standardised or automated tasks, and on particular parts of the law firm value chain, where a sophisticated IT structure and efficient processes are regarded as a competitive advantage. More and more companies are sending the more standardised or automated tasks to alternative providers, or are convincing their law firms of choice to outsource such work. But when it comes to medium and high-end tasks, law firms are still the natural choice. For now. There are already alternative providers striving to move up the value chain, and more and more are competing directly with law firms.

Who drives innovation and change

Irrespective of the actual market penetration of alternative providers, the existence of new providers with innovative business models is undoubtedly a growing phenomenon. The existence of innovative ideas, new business or delivery models, and alternative providers is perhaps a necessary condition for innovation and radical change in the legal market, but it is hardly a sufficient cause. What really drives innovation and change is the necessity or the sheer pressure to be innovative.

Being innovative is not a 'lifestyle decision'. Only companies that are ultimately paying the bills of both law firms and alternative providers need to find innovative ways to deliver legal services. Hence, there is a pressure on general counsel to find new ways to deliver legal services to the company. Mostly this pressure comes directly from the CFO or the CEO.

Legal departments are under pressure to fundamentally change the way in which they deliver legal services to their company; hence, they will increasingly pile the pressure both on law firms and alternative providers to deliver added value and to come up with radically different ways to deliver legal services. General counsel are in the driver's seat when it comes to future developments in the legal industry, and they will determine the direction in which the market is headed, and ultimately the future of both law firms and alternative providers. Without a direct, identifiable benefit for the companies involved, the good ideas behind every major innovation will remain no more than that: ideas.

Core hypotheses derived from the study

In the course of the study, we developed some overall hypotheses on the future of the legal market in general, and on the future of the three market participants. The legal market is currently in a flux and significant changes are starting to happen. Alternative providers are something new to the legal market and they are absolutely here to stay. But they need to prove their added value over a long period of time to really become a serious threat to law firms (as true competitors) and legal departments (as a real alternative to traditional law firms).

The most important driver for change for now is IT: what can be done through IT and software will be done through IT and software (even if quality levels are slightly lower). This opens up room for alternative providers, as traditional law firms often lack the required knowledge and energy when it comes to accomplishing tasks in the most efficient way.

The question of disruption is of second order – it is a (slow) evolutionary development towards a more nuanced landscape of different legal providers, meeting more specifically articulated client needs.

Legal departments need time to adjust to the new provider landscape; hence, only alternative providers who pursue a long-term strategy will succeed in the long-run. General counsel will continue to profoundly test and question every new service or business model to establish if it can really add value. Hence, more innovative delivery models that were very recently initiated are of course interesting, but the broad market proof of concept is still pending. Long-established alternative providers are increasingly and successfully becoming integrated into the market – particularly the insourcing market segment has turned out to be a very profitable (niche) market. Simultaneously, alternative providers are trying to move up the value chain ('managed legal services') and succeed in the first lighthouse projects.

The use of alternative providers should not be overrated, however; developing a brand is a long-haul exercise, a marathon rather than a sprint, and law firms will only be partially threatened by alternative providers. High-end legal advice remains the home turf of big law, but low/medium work and 2nd/3rd tier law firms will be severely impacted. Law firms, not known as disruptors themselves, should more actively embrace the opportunities this new environment offers

– even considering to acquire an alternative provider. Be that as it may, law firms still enjoy the extremely powerful position as the first point of call when it comes to legal or regulatory issues. They should leverage this hallowed position as long as they have the opportunity to do so: for as long as it takes alternative service providers to develop a similar position of strength.

About the authors

Markus Hartung is a lawyer and mediator. He is director of the Bucerius Center on the Legal Profession (CLP) at Bucerius Law School, Hamburg. He has a broad experience in managing law firms. In 1999, he was elected as managing partner of Oppenhoff & Rädler. During his tenure, he oversaw the firm's merger with Linklaters and served as the managing partner of Linklaters in Germany from 2001–2008 and as a member of the global executive committee of Linklaters.

At the CLP, he focuses on legal market research and is responsible for the conception of educational and continuing education programmes (management and leadership) for legal professionals. His particular expertise lies in market development and trends, management and strategic leadership, as well as corporate governance of law firms, combined with the regulatory requirements of various legal markets. Since 2007, he has been a member of the Committee on Professional Regulation of the German Bar Association, chairing this committee since January 2011.

As a lawyer, Markus focuses on conflict management, regulatory issues, and professional indemnity issues. In addition, he advises law firms in strategy and management questions and coaches partners in management functions.

He is a regular conference speaker on leadership, management topics, and professional ethics, and has written numerous articles and book chapters on these topics. He is co-editor and author of *Der Rechtsmarkt in Deutschland* (The Legal Market in Germany), which came to the market in early 2014, and which has developed into a standard reference for the German legal market.

Arne Gärtner is research assistant at the Bucerius Center on the Legal Profession (CLP) at Bucerius Law School, Hamburg. From 2005 to 2011, he studied business administration at the University of Potsdam. He specialised in the fields of professional service firms and entrepreneurship/innovation management and graduated with a diploma in business administration (comp. M.Sc.). From 2013 to 2015, Arne studied mediation at the European University Viadrina and graduated with a Master of Arts (MA). He is also a trained mediator.

His research at the Bucerius CLP focuses on the value of legal services from corporations' point of view, innovation, and change management in law firms and legal departments, and also on the competitive environment of the legal market in general. At the University of Potsdam, he is currently writing a dissertation on 'Legal departments of large corporations – efficient and effective organisation and management'.

Reference

1. Clayton M. Christensen introduced the term 'disruptive technologies' in 1995, and has written several books on disruptive innovation. He is widely recognised as the expert in this field.

Chapter 2: Building a culture of innovation in legal services

By Adam Billing, partner, and Abigail Hunt, associate, at Møller PSF Group

The innovation imperative

The trends that are driving change in the legal sector are well known: clients demanding more for less, the billable hour under fire, shifting workforce demographics, the growing need for global reach. These trends are all exacerbated by new technologies that enable, among other things, greater legal process outsourcing, e-discovery, and virtual working. All of these factors, combined with new client needs and regulatory changes, create an environment ripe for disruption in terms of how legal services are delivered, what those services might include, as well as who is delivering them.

At the present time, the greatest impetus for change in legal services is coming from in-house legal teams. These teams are under pressure to deliver both more and different strategic value to their own changing businesses.

Des Woods, chairman and a founding partner of the Møller PSF Group at Cambridge University, said 'Clients complain constantly that their legal suppliers are behind the game in terms of innovating around service delivery and pricing. Their view is that most innovation is in the in-house lawyer community, as they face direct budget pressure from their boards. Having said that, the market has definitely woken up and many, but not all, firm leaders are gearing up for major change.'

How long will it take to reach a tipping point when some law firms will be forced to change their model? And how long before innovation is at the top of the agenda for more than just the most forward-looking firms?

Greg Bott, head of the Client Development Centre for Addleshaw Goddard LLP, commented: 'The improving economy might have been detrimental to the rise of innovation – hiding some of the issues and cracks. A slight cooling may help unearth those things that need to be addressed.'

Exactly how the legal services landscape will evolve over the coming years is far from certain. What is definite, however, is that innovation will play a central role in this evolution.

A culture of innovation

With some notable exceptions, much of the innovation that has taken place in the legal sector has been what can be described as 'spot innovation'. These are innovations that occur in response to a particular client

Legal sector innovation

Over the last few years, legal sector innovation has received increasing attention in the media and from a growing number of awards bodies. New service, product, strategy, and process innovations have in many cases been driven by advances in technology that are transforming the way work is managed and delivered, both externally and internally.

request, regulatory change, or internal business challenge – not the result of a strategic and coordinated effort to drive growth and profitability through innovation.

While these successes should not be undervalued, innovation in legal services is still rarely taking place at the level required to take full advantage of the opportunities ahead and to cope with the magnitude of change and uncertainty building within the sector. This requires a more systemic and intentional approach than currently exists in most firms today. It requires a 'culture of innovation'.

In recent years, 'creating a culture of innovation' has become a frequently cited strategic objective for businesses of all kinds. But what does that really mean? We define a culture of innovation as the collective practices, mindsets, policies, and norms that enable an organisation to make innovation part of business as usual. In this type of culture, innovation is a core, constant activity of the organisation – as opposed to something that is done in addition to the 'real' work of the firm.

When a culture of innovation is in place, the firm is inherently better able to identify new opportunities as they emerge, think creatively about how to respond, and mobilise resources to rapidly develop and implement solutions. Specifically, this results in:

- Greater agility and responsiveness to change;
- Improved collaboration across the firm, with clients and other parties;
- Profitable new revenue streams and internal cost savings;
- Improved employee engagement and productivity; and
- Increased growth potential and competitive advantage.

How this manifests will vary widely from firm to firm. There is no one-size-fits-all solution – nor are there transferrable templates to follow. Organisational strategy, structure, history, and innovation objectives all have a profound effect on the shape a firm's culture of innovation needs to take to be effective.

However, from our experience of working in the professional services and corporate sectors, a number of lessons learned and key success factors have emerged that can help

Legal sector innovation in action: External strategies

Externally focused innovations include new legal strategies, such as Simmons & Simmons' creation of a cost and time saving strategy to redirect PPI litigation away from the courts, and instead into its clients' internal complaint-handling functions. Or novel service offerings, such as Hogan Lovells' creation of the Privacy Innovation Assessment, a tool that helps clients assess the privacy implications of new business developments and recommends practical steps to address them.

Legal sector innovation in action: Alternative service providers

AdventBalance, a young Australian firm offering fixed rates, lawyer pools, and a unique staffing arrangement, whereby top-tier experienced lawyers work directly in client businesses on a secondment basis, has enjoyed double and even triple digit growth rates in the last five years. Schillings reorganised itself entirely when it moved to ABS status and repositioned itself as a multi-disciplinary firm offering a comprehensive reputation defence package made up of consultancy services, cyber security services, and legal assistance. Since the change, the firm's revenue has climbed by 30 per cent.

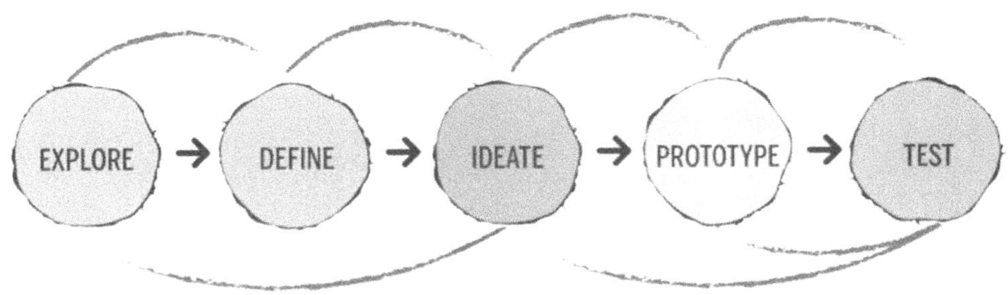

Figure 1: Design thinking – An innovation framework

law firms create an innovation culture that produces the desired results, while avoiding some of the most common pitfalls.

Create the foundation – Building skills and awareness

The bedrock of a strong innovation culture is a shared understanding of how innovation works and the business case for doing it. This requires a common framework that everyone can easily grasp, apply, and practise – forming the basis for a common language and approach for how innovation happens in the firm.

Legal sector innovation in action: Internal strategies

In the realm of internal innovation, there is a move towards more flexible time arrangements, as well as the provision of more structured training in areas beyond law, such as wider commercial skills for junior associates. Allen & Overy made the move to flexible working in 2010 and Linklaters allows lawyers to work from home one day per week as of this year. Simmons & Simmons has been recognised for its internal innovations, including the launch of its own MBA course in partnership with BPP business school, designed to prepare a new generation of lawyers with a range of legal and business skills.

Creating this foundation requires an investment in developing people from across the firm – not just fee earners or senior leaders.

Design thinking – A unifying framework for innovation

In recent years, a growing number of law schools and firms have looked to 'design thinking' to equip lawyers and law students with the process, tools, and mindsets required to successfully innovate for their clients and within their firms.

Design thinking, an innovation framework used by some of the world's most consistently cutting edge companies, gives people a straightforward, practical approach to creative problem solving that can be applied to virtually any challenge (see Figure 1).

It starts by seeking to deeply understand what people (e.g. clients or internal customers) really value, need, and care about, and it applies a creative process and toolset to arrive at more innovative solutions for the challenges they face. Individuals trained in this approach learn how to use techniques such as effective questioning and empathy building, opportunity framing, brainstorming, and lateral thinking, as well as rapid prototyping and experimentation.

With these core skills and mindsets instilled, every individual in the firm can be part of the innovation process. They become 'listening posts' for opportunities to innovate both for clients and internal stakeholders. They also become more confident in suggesting new ideas, secure in the knowledge that others understand the importance of deferring judgment and building on the ideas of others. Meetings tend to become more focused on action and rapid iteration, rather than endless updates, and discussion and collaboration between disciplines become more fluid due to a shared toolset and approach to problem solving.

For many organisations, the most immediate benefits of equipping people with an innovative framework and toolkit like design thinking come from the way these techniques are applied in day-to-day work. Small changes to the way individuals and teams organise and manage themselves can have a profound effect on the quality of work and the speed at which it is accomplished.

Making innovation skills development count

Leadership development and structured training can be powerful tools in building a culture of innovation, but there are several common pitfalls to avoid.

1. Don't just develop senior people.

What often happens is that a small cohort of senior leaders will go away for a day or so of innovation training and return to an organisation that is not only oblivious to the concepts that they have learned, but in some cases geared to stamp them out. This makes applying and disseminating any of these new ideas very difficult, and despite best intentions, organisational inertia takes over and the status quo prevails.

Another problem with rolling these skills out to only a small group of senior leaders is that while their buy-in is required to establish a culture of innovation, it is not enough. The real work of innovation takes place on the front lines. These individuals also need to be engaged and on board before any real progress can be expected.

Legal sector innovation in action: IT-driven innovation

In terms of IT-driven innovation, firms have used technology not only to reduce time and costs though automation, but also to enhance communication and facilitate collaboration, especially across offices. For example, Berwin Leighton Paisner has been able to assume responsibility for all the legal needs of some of its clients under multi-year, fixed-price agreements because it has built a multi-sourcing platform that supports BLP onsite teams. Technological innovations are also helping firms to provide longer term, more predictable fee estimates. Paul Hastings was recognised this year for its development and deployment of a matter management system that improves efficiency and helps to give predictable fee estimates to clients.

2. Don't just develop a small group of front-line innovators.

For many organisations, there is a temptation to invest heavily in developing the innovative capabilities of just a small group who will be tasked with driving innovation in the firm. These are frequently those people who are deemed to be 'the innovative ones'– and could be partners or associates who have been flagged as future leaders or high potentials.

These groups are often tasked with projects, which when launched have strong top leadership support. But as projects continue, team members often face pressure from direct line managers to spend more time on their 'real jobs' and are pulled away, resulting in stalled projects and disheartened would-be innovators.

Another danger of only developing small cohorts is that the way they will be working often won't make sense to their colleagues, and will therefore be rejected. Worse still, they may seek to involve senior people who haven't bought in to the value of seemingly counter-intuitive concepts like fast failure and rapid prototyping, and so end up getting criticised or 'marked down' as a result.

Development initiatives are absolutely key to building a culture of innovation, but making them count takes real commitment. Not everyone in the firm needs to become an 'innovation expert', but virtually everyone needs to possess basic awareness of a shared framework, understand how innovation aligns with the business strategy, and be ready to support and encourage others.

What kind of innovation do you want?

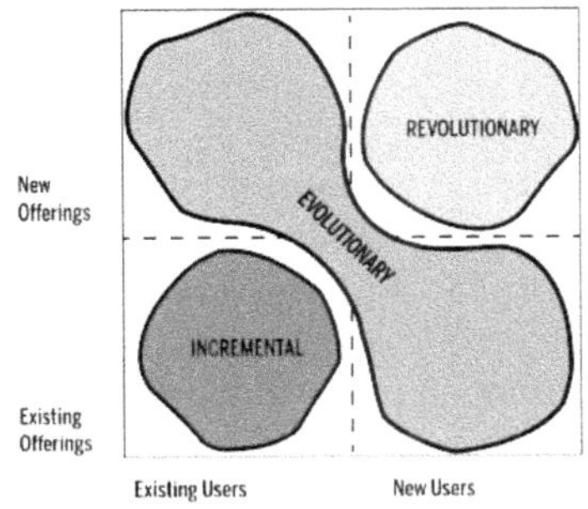

Figure 2: Categorising innovation – Incremental, evolutionary, or revolutionary?

Knowing what kind of innovation will be most important for your firm can help inform the type of culture you need to achieve it, and the practical steps you need to take to build and sustain it. One simple way to look at different types of innovation is to divide them in to incremental, evolutionary, and revolutionary (see Figure 2).

Incremental innovations involve making changes to an existing service that is being delivered to an existing client. Examples of this might be a change in the way a service is priced or an added feature on an existing product. These innovations tend to be relatively low risk, and with little disruptive potential.

Evolutionary innovations involve diving into a new market or new product or service type. The firm might be entering adjacent markets, combining elements where the firm has existing expertise or relationships with others that are entirely new to it. Here, the risks as well as the potential for rewards are increased. Examples from the legal sector include Bird & Bird's Baseline and DLA Piper's Noble Street, where the firms offer non-legal advisory services in familiar markets.

Finally, there is the top right quadrant: revolutionary innovation. Here, the firm might be making a radical move into an entirely new service sector where the firm has no real experience. Innovations of this type are extremely high risk (often associated with greater than 90 per cent failure rates), but have the highest potential for market disruption if they are successful.

Depending on your strategy and risk appetite, your firm may tend towards one end of this spectrum more than another.

Provide the right time, space, and funding

David Halliwell, director of knowledge, risk, and legal services for Pinsent Masons LLP, commented: 'Partners get out of bed to solve clients' problems, and those go beyond the specific transaction or need for advice in front of them. Where partners have time and space to think – and a client-led incentive to deliver – then innovation flies.'

Without making time to innovate, innovation is not likely to happen – at least not in any deliberate, reliable way. But what is the best way to do this in the time-starved environments of most law firms? Strategies such as allowing a certain percentage of time per week to innovate have gained popularity, following examples from companies like Google and others of that ilk. However, our experience working with organisations that have implemented similar policies tells us that this approach often fails because:

a) It is never fully implemented;
b) Top leadership support isn't sustained;
c) People lack the skills and tools to use the time in a useful way; or
d) It is slowly eroded away by other projects that inevitably take higher priority.

Allowing time to innovate means allowing time to reflect – which in turn means removing high-priority tasks from the already overflowing plates of most fee earners and support staff. Perhaps, one day, time spent on innovation will carry the same weight as meeting ambitious billing targets and deadlines for urgent client work. Until this happens, most law firms, and most corporates for that matter, are going to need to find other ways to make innovation happen.

Making innovation teams work

From our experience, even in organisations where innovation is widely encouraged at the individual level, there is no substitute for dedicated innovation teams when it comes to delivering on the full promise of innovation.

Innovation teams might be formed of members drawn from across the firm on a rotation basis. The innovation project might, but does not need to be, the sole priority of members for a period of several weeks to multiple months. At the most basic level, successful innovation teams require:

1. **A clear brief** – A well-framed opportunity and definition of what is in scope, what is not, and under what conditions the project should be extended or dropped.
2. **Sufficient funding** – There is also no better way to demonstrate the firm's commitment to innovation than to visibly put real resources behind it. At the outset, make a budget available that is commensurate with the potential upside of the project, but encourage teams to develop the project through frequent low cost experiments that lead to more developed pilots as learning is incorporated in each iteration.
3. **Diverse membership** – The best teams are comprised of a people with wide and varied skill sets from across practices, sectors, and offices – and not just lawyers. They might include business services people, administrators and managers, as well as clients and other contacts from outside the firm.
4. **A process to guide them** – Innovation teams will struggle to make real progress using their traditional ways of working. Having a structured process to guide their thinking and working will improve outcomes and the ability for diverse teams to quickly and fluidly collaborate.
5. **A dedicated space for the project to live** – Even if it is a space as humble as a single conference room or the corner of an office space, innovation projects tend to be more successful when teams have a fixed physical space to go to where they can be immersed in the project.
6. **A hands-off management approach** – Innovation teams need to be managed and rewarded differently than teams focused on the core business of the firm. This requires a good deal of trust, empowerment, and permission to fail as long as the learning from that failure is captured and applied to ensuring the next iteration is closer to success.
7. **Measurement that fits the task** – A team working on a 'revolutionary' innovation project (see Figure 2) shouldn't be measured in the same way as a team working on an incremental innovation,

which has a far higher chance of success and is much closer to the firm's core business. Teams on high-risk projects could be rewarded, for example, not only for the success achieved, but also for the valuable lessons captured and shared with teams working on less risky projects.

Perhaps most importantly, successful innovation teams require the rest of the firm, especially senior leadership, to be on board with the team's purpose and the process they are using. This is the best way to ensure that the required time will be made available and respected in spite of competing priorities. Broad awareness and buy-in can also greatly reduce the risk of teams' interim work products and methods being evaluated by traditional measures and potentially getting quashed before they get off the ground.

Recognise common barriers to innovation

Innovation is not easy for anyone. It can create a fear of change and a resulting pulling up of the drawbridge. Actively or passively resisting change is, for some people, much more comfortable than managing the uncertainty that comes with something new.

Innovation can be especially hard for law firms with their business model still largely based on partner ownership, the billable hour, often strict hierarchies, and a long history of practising law and running their business in a certain way. While there are no easy fixes, and change in most of these areas will be slow at best, it is vital to actively anticipate these roadblocks to innovation and use levers such as incentives, performance measurement systems, remuneration policy, and inspiring leadership to address them over time.

The billable hour

Innovation requires an 'outside-in' mentality where the client is at the heart of the firm's strategy and service delivery model. The billable hour model is an example of 'inside-out' thinking that is driven by what the firm is providing to the client as opposed to what they are creating for them or helping them achieve.

Andrew Giverin, sales director at Radiant Law, commented: 'From the client's point of view the legal sector is crying out for innovation. Everything pegged to billable hours encourages inefficiency. The billable hour is based on input not output or the value of what is generated. This makes it difficult to generate innovative ideas.'

From this perspective, as well as in terms of measuring and rewarding innovation activities, the billable hour model presents significant challenges. A fee-earner's performance is primarily measured by billing levels, and innovation work is most often non-billable. In a delivery-focused culture, this creates a major hurdle for securing the time, resources, and support required to make innovation happen.

Hierarchies and power pockets

As well as the pressure of billable hours on lawyers, there is almost always an entrenched hierarchy in place, based on title, expertise, billing power, and years of post-qualification experience. Sometimes, as is the case within many groups of people, alliances and pockets of power can be partly hidden. For example, close colleagues who have moved en masse from other firms, friendships based on decades of working together, and cliques cemented by, say, godchildren or golf.

Innovation requires, if not a flat structure, a flat mentality that sets aside rank, role, and history. With partners at the top of decision-making tree, it may take real effort to create an environment, even if just a temporary one, where the ideas of a junior lawyer or business services manager have equal weight to those of a senior partner. It is, after all, not always the most senior people in the firm that will have the most revealing insights into emerging client needs or where internal process or cost efficiencies might be found.

Short-termism

Law firm leaders have to balance partner pressure for maximum short-term profit share against longer-term investment in innovation. Convincing partners exactly why they should care about and invest in innovation requires a compelling vision and strategy for success in both the short and long term.

Client feedback, client requests, and a changing share of the client purse add weight here. In addition, regular competitive analysis, working to stay attuned to likely future market shifts, and monitoring trends in other sectors that might impact on longer-term service demand can help to reinforce the link between current innovation initiatives and future competitive advantage.

Bias for precision

Almost everything about the training and professional standing of lawyers encourages 'getting things right', a fear of failure, and an aversion to making mistakes. Innovation requires most lawyers to change their mind-set or, metaphorically, to put on a different hat. Being able to flex between cautious, detail-oriented legal thinking and more risk-friendly and 'bigger picture', innovation-related thinking requires self-awareness, sustained effort, and encouragement. Failure, when it inevitably happens, must not be seen as an 'end', but rather a necessary step in an iterative process, and it must be recognised as a means of ultimately achieving success sooner.

Organisational structure

Here, structure is not only the central partnership model but also the systems and levers that make the business work – the groups, the hierarchy, reporting structure, information and decision making channels, reward and promotion systems.

Innovation requires collaboration – and lots of it. Collaboration can be especially powerful when teams are drawn from diverse backgrounds, allowing for fresh perspectives and solutions to emerge. Not all firms are structured in a way that enables great collaboration. In fact, some seem to be set up to almost deliberately encourage silos and internal competition, and collaborating across practice area or offices is often both difficult and frustrating. Such barriers may exist due to implicit norms around sharing of information, cross-practice tension, cultural differences, a by-product of the reward system, or the 'not invented here' mentality.

However, structure can also play to a firm's advantage. Cross-disciplinary collaboration is one of the benefits that can come from taking a sector-based approach – something claimed by many firms yet achieved by just a few.

Christian Bartsch, Partner at Bird & Bird LLP, said: 'The culture at Bird & Bird is underpinned by a shared sense of natural curiosity. Our deep sector focus means that our lawyers are truly passionate about their sectors, sector-based budgeting encourages strong collaboration and our clients tend to be highly innovative themselves.'

Lead by example and others will follow

Without leadership support, any effort to build a robust culture of innovation is very likely to fail. Influencing something as hard to pin down and measure as law firm culture requires committed and consistent leadership action in deeds as well as declarations. It takes a willingness to empower people across all levels of the firm, take risks, and accept and even embrace the ambiguity that comes with venturing into uncharted territory.

While there are many attributes that a strong leader of innovation needs to possess, in our experience, there is none more powerful, or indispensable, than being a clear and visible role model. Creating and maintaining a culture of innovation requires unequivocal leadership modelling by law firm leadership and management teams on a day-to-day basis. This is a universe away from well-intentioned lip service and an annual innovation awards event. Innovation has to become a visible and integral part of business as usual from the top down.

Being a role model for innovation involves sharing regular and credible evidence of your commitment to promoting the best thinking of your people, to support them when they try in earnest and sometimes fail, and to publically recognise them when their efforts bear fruit as learning or progress in whatever form.

Without trust that their innovation-related mindsets and behaviours will be welcomed rather than penalised, your talented workforce will likely:

- Continue to sit on potentially valuable ideas;
- Hold back their strong views and insights;
- Feel under-confident about discussing innovation with clients (leaving space for competitors to do so);
- Become frustrated and weaker ambassadors for your brand; and
- Be less inclined to collaborate internally and with clients towards creative and more innovative solutions.

This all adds up to a significant loss of competitive advantage. By showing, through body language, words, and deeds, and on a day-to-day basis, exactly how vital innovation is to the business, senior leaders can model the message a thousand times more effectively than any number of board papers, emails, or glossy brochures ever could.

Successful innovation necessitates a 'do as I do', not a 'do as I say' leadership style.

Conclusion: Building a culture of innovation

If you and your firm are already building a culture of innovation, be sure to do it well. This is no subject for a shiny veneer or superficial commitment. Culture change is never fast or painless. However, creating an environment where innovation happens in a continuous, strategically aligned way can have a profound impact on a firm's long-term profitability and growth potential – especially in times of accelerating change.

From our experience, this requires funding and actively supporting *both* firm-wide development initiatives *and* dedicated team-based innovation projects simultaneously. Omitting one dramatically limits the effectiveness of the other. When done together, they are mutually reinforcing. It also compels firms to take a close and honest look at those aspects of their existing culture, structure, and leadership style that might help or hinder a culture of innovation – and take meaningful steps to address them. Finally, law firms need to be open to learning from other sectors, and willing to adopt and adapt the right practices and frameworks in a way that is compatible with their uniquely delivery-focused and standards-driven environments.

David Halliwell, director of knowledge, risk and legal services for Pinsent Masons LLP, said '... law firms are the last businesses in the supply chain to be transformed. But being last is not such a bad thing. Law firms can learn quickly from other sectors and bring mainstream concepts newly to law to make business-changing progress quickly.'

The time is now. Don't procrastinate. Take small steps right now and fast – the advantages are enormous.

The ripple effect: Broader implications of an innovation culture

Innovation is relevant to every aspect of the business – not just to the development of new products and services or IT systems. As a culture of innovation grows within a firm, many of the practices and norms that we take for granted are likely to evolve along the way. Changes you might expect include, but are not limited to:

- The way you inspire, develop, empower, and reward your people;
- Greater likelihood of involving colleagues and clients in the very early stages of designing new products and services;
- The way people in the firm ask questions, actively listen and observe, and provide feedback;
- Communicating value, scope, and pricing options clearly and in a way that meets agreed rather than assumed client needs;
- Your style of leadership and management approach;
- Greater attention paid to the innovations of competitors, including new entrants who have based their entire model on technology, client service, and innovation;
- The way you collaborate internally and externally, including investing time in building diverse networks and listening to different perspectives;
- The way you encourage ideas, manage expectations about how they will be used, develop prototypes, and respond to 'failure';
- Greater appetite to learn from other sectors about trends and different ways of doing things;
- Overcoming the tendency to hold on to work that can, over time, be more profitably and efficiently done elsewhere or in a different way;
- Having greater leadership support or authority to move at speed to capitalise on small-window opportunities to meet client needs ahead of competitors; and
- Ensuring that everyone in the firm understands their part in the bigger picture – the link between their work and the specific client benefit.

What changes might you expect to see in your firm?

About the authors

Adam Billing is a partner in Møller PSF Group Cambridge (www.mollerpsfgcambridge.com) and founder of innovation consultancy TreeHouse (www.treehouseinnovation.com). Abigail Hunt is an associate in Møller PSF Group Cambridge and a senior associate in TreeHouse. Both work with leading corporate and professional service organisations, helping them to develop new products, services, and strategy, and to build their own internal innovative capacity. With thanks to colleagues Garth Olcese and Duncan Brannan.

Chapter 3: Developing knowledge capability to support innovation

By Mark Gould, founder of Mark Gould Consulting

INNOVATION IS rooted in knowledge, combined with creativity and imagination. This combination is also critical to good legal advice: helping clients achieve their goals within the constraints imposed by the law. Unlike legal advice, however, transformative innovations may not have easily identifiable client demand. Deep change also depends on the firm itself being geared towards innovation as a core activity, rather than relying on ideas being generated randomly.

Innovative people will always have good ideas. The real challenge for law firms is to cultivate innovation better. That has two parts:

- Transforming people and teams that cannot or will not innovate so that they come up with new ideas; and
- Taking ideas from all sources and developing them into marketable products or services.

Creating a culture within which innovation is a natural expectation for all in the firm is a hard task. To achieve that goal, firms need to think differently about knowledge.

Innovation basics

Innovation doesn't take place in a vacuum. In order to be of any use, good ideas have to be recognised and valued by someone other than the person with the idea. In most cases this will be clients, but the firm itself might be the intended beneficiary. Truly useful changes are marked by the value they bring. 'Innovation' is best thought of as 'an improvement that meets a real need'. That need might be external (improving client service, for example) or internal (where a change in working practices results in improvements to profit).

For these purposes, the possible improvements that firms might make can be separated into four types:

- Innovation in the law itself (providing a novel legal solution to client's legal or business problem);
- New products or services developed for clients at the practice group level;
- Improvements that completely change the way the firm works with clients (client service delivery); and
- Improvements in the way the firm runs that are invisible to clients (internal operations).

Of these types of innovation, the first depends on an explicit client need and simply requires an imaginative lawyer to act on the opportunity presented by the client. Such innovations could occur in any firm. The others require the firm to be supportive of experimentation (not all ideas succeed) and change (successful initiatives require old ways of working to be put aside).

Traditional law firms often find it hard to tolerate experimentation and change, especially when they have an annual cycle of budgeting and investment. New forms of legal business, which can often take a longer view, may have a greater capacity for innovation as a result. Resistance to experimentation also explains why a small number of business-focused changes (legal project management, different pricing models, use of paralegals and other resourcing models) occur in a large number of firms. These improvements are based on business practices outside the law, and have been proven in use. As firms see them introduced elsewhere, they can see the benefits in action and copy their peers.

Whatever innovation process a firm has, there will be some key stages that depend heavily on knowledge and knowledge-related skills. The following are particularly worthy of note:

- Generation of ideas;
- Assessment of likely impact of the new idea (whatever form it might take); and
- Evaluation of possible market reaction.

Each of these stages demands different types of knowledge or insight, mobilised in different ways. That knowledge or insight may contribute to the idea itself, the need for the improvement, or both. Firms wanting a more innovative culture therefore need to concentrate on fostering the right knowledge activities and habits.

Table 1 shows more precisely the kinds of questions firms may need to answer by drawing on knowledge.

Knowledge management and innovation

Left to their own devices, good lawyers will always come up with good new ways of working with their clients. Better, more consistent results come when the firm has established tools, techniques, and processes to make it easier for good lawyers to follow their instincts and for others to reach the standard of the good ones. No modern law firm should rely solely on the instincts of their people – they need to intervene to improve performance. That is one of the core functions of knowledge management (KM) in law firms.

Law firms have traditionally approached KM by concentrating on gathering and improving access to legal know-how and lawyers' expertise and experience. This kind of legal KM ensures that lawyers can do work of the same type more effectively on successive occasions. That leads to the creation of resources such as banks of standard documents, training programmes, know-how repositories, search engines, and expertise locators. Those things will always remain important, and may themselves be the subject of innovation (by using established knowledge more intelligently in the form of automated documents, client self-service products, and so on).

KM activities of this type are inherently backward-looking. They capture historic activities and present them to lawyers as a guide for future use. If that future use is identical to the past, the resource in question will obviously be valuable. If the future use is dissimilar, but the lawyer is intelligent, the resource may be helpful as a guide. Traditional KM resources can therefore help support the generation of ideas in response to client need. This is because those ideas depend heavily on what lawyers know about the law itself. They can also help lawyers assess how successful the idea might be in achieving the client's goals, as that might be underpinned by an understanding of previous court decisions or successful negotiating positions. Those facts might be noted in a good KM system, or other experts within the firm (identified using an expertise locator, for example) might be able to provide the requisite guidance.

Once clients have been advised on novel legal issues, that information should find its way into the firm's knowledge system. If other clients bring similar queries, the knowledge system should be updated with more detailed information about the topic – perhaps even including standard

	Ideas	Impact	Reaction
Legal solutions	What knowledge do we have to solve novel client problems?	What do we know to help judge the likely success of solutions we propose?	Do we have enough experience and distinctive knowledge to found a new practice area?
Products/services	Which know-how is most suitable for packaging, and what kind of delivery mechanisms are possible?	Do clients want this – is there a need and does it fit with their existing systems?	What is the future for this product or service? How can we sustain it or develop it when it is copied?
Client service	How could we meet our clients' needs better? What do we know about what might be within our (legal and other) capabilities?	What are our clients' needs (not just those expressed directly, but also those implicit in their behaviour and market context)?	What are the implications for the firm if we are successful in changing the way we deliver client service? How might the market react and what else might need to change?
Internal operations	Where do we perform well, and where poorly? What could be different?	What are our needs (not just those expressed directly, but also those implicit in our behaviour and market context)?	What are the implications for the firm if we are successful in changing the way it works? How might the market react, and what else might need to change?

Table 1: Questions that draw on knowledge to drive innovation

documents or anonymised examples of client advice. As it becomes clearer that there is an appreciable market for advice of this type, a new practice group might be established. The development and success of this group would depend on a number of things, including the existence of critical knowledge resources. The knowledge system therefore contributes to an assessment of and reaction to market needs.

This sequence of events provides an example of the first type of legal innovation. It also matches Richard Susskind's now well-known description of the evolution of legal services. Novel advice is initially bespoke to a particular client, but then becomes standardised with repetition, and then systematised into a new practice area. All these steps take place within the firm. Clients will benefit, but there may be no fundamental change in the way they are serviced by the firm. The next stage in Susskind's description (the packaging of legal advice) is also supported by traditional KM, but its impact is more obvious to clients. In being packaged, firms' legal insight is turned into products or services that clients can use without instructing a lawyer.

Using existing knowledge from within the firm to create new legal services or products might represent an improvement to clients, but legal knowledge alone is insufficient for innovation of this type. In order to transcend existing distillations of legal knowledge, such as bulletins, briefings, or training sessions, a new product or service needs to be packaged in a novel fashion. This might mean using an existing delivery mechanism in a new way or using a completely new method. Selecting the right approach will often depend on insight that lawyers do not have. Instead, firms will need to use non-legal knowledge that is not usually found in their KM systems.

Examples of this kind of innovation abound in the law – long-standing examples include the Out-Law service from Masons (now Pinsent Masons) and Linklaters' online term sheet generator. Each of these embedded existing legal knowledge practices within novel forms of delivery so that clients (and others) could use the firm's know-how without a lawyer acting as intermediary.

Traditional KM activities support the development of creative legal solutions for individual clients and their evolution into standalone practice areas. However, firms need additional input to create more wide-ranging innovations. This is true for packaged products and services – while lawyers are well placed to decide that certain content is ripe for packaging, it is increasingly unlikely that they will be the best people to decide the form that package (the delivery mechanism) should take.

A focus on legal material also means that traditional KM is incapable of helping firms judge the likelihood of success of a novel product or service by reference to whether or not it meets client needs. If an innovation of this type is successful with clients, other firms in the market will react by copying it or by innovating in different directions. Legal KM can't help firms plan how to respond to those market reactions.

In general, then, the approach to knowledge management adopted by most law firms can only assist with the most basic innovations. Firms that want to do something genuinely new above and beyond this level have to approach knowledge differently. In particular, they need to learn how to access the less visible knowledge within the firm and combine it with other insights to create something that hasn't existed before.

A different approach: Improving knowledge capability

Innovations in client service delivery and internal operations fundamentally change the way a firm works. Such changes need to be rooted in a deep understanding of the firm and its market, its clients and their markets, and broader technical environmental issues. This demands an approach to knowledge that goes beyond KM as firms have traditionally understood it. Such an approach has been defined by David Griffiths (a specialist in this area) as knowledge capability:

> *'... the ability to deploy knowledge to constantly design, develop, deliver, and maintain products and/or services that its current and future stakeholders will find valuable – put another way, an organisation's Knowledge Capability is an indicator of its adaptive capability (its ability to anticipate (sense) and react to change)'.*

As described already, traditional KM tends to concentrate on gathering and redeploying what is already known. This is an answer-focused approach. A standard document or practice note is defined in part by the purposes to which it will be put. It is presented as an answer to predictable questions. In addition, good lawyers might use KM material as indirect aids in unpredicted but comparable situations.

Other KM resources have a similar function. For example, lawyer profiles in an expertise database are written with existing needs in mind – they provide possible answers to questions that are already understood, such as 'who is our expert in this area of law?' They work less well when the questions are more unexpected, such as 'how can we work better with clients in this novel sector?'

It is essential that firms have these traditional answer-focused resources at the foundation of their knowledge strategy. Without them, there would be too many inefficiencies for the firm to survive, let alone be in a position to assist clients with novel legal problems. However, the state of the legal market now means that mere survival is not enough. In the face of intensified competition, client pressure on fees and performance, and regulatory change, no firm can thrive merely by doing what it currently does more efficiently.

Unlike traditional KM activities, frameworks for developing knowledge capability tend to prioritise questions rather than answers. This is a cultural change as much as an organisational strategy. In order for a firm to make the most of a question-focused approach, a number of characteristics are needed. The most important of these are connectivity, openness, and trust.

We have already seen how connections within a firm can assist in producing useful ideas. When considering packaging legal knowledge into new products and services, lawyers depend on the insight of others in the firm. These could include technologists, marketers, learning professionals, or anyone who might have a fresh perspective on what would help clients. At present, these connections have to be made deliberately: the lawyer needs to be aware of someone who could help and ask them directly. A better approach would be to improve the general level of awareness of work that is being done across the firm so that people can volunteer their help when they see that it might be needed. Firms that ensure that all their people can see what is being done for clients (within the bounds of confidentiality), and encourage the general sharing of insights of all types, are more likely to see a higher rate of successful innovations. In all areas of life and work, novel ideas often occur when someone sees something in an unrelated area that resonates in their own.

Better connectivity across the firm is an essential starting point for improving knowledge capability. However, the improved connections need to have some substance in them. Like electrical cables or water pipes, they need to be filled with something that can flow around the firm. Within a firm, good connections between people improve the flow of information. That information could be anything that is even tangentially relevant to the firm's work. It would certainly include information about clients and their sectors, but for maximum value firms also need to be transparent about more sensitive things like financial data at a fairly detailed level, or unedited feedback provided by clients.

When people have greater visibility of the firm's performance and reflections about the work done across the firm, sometimes known as 'working out loud', they can make better informed decisions about their own work. They can also offer support to others when previously they might not have known that their assistance would have been useful. Without openness and transparency, those opportunities for innovation are unavailable.

Two strands of technological development are notable for improving connectivity and openness. Improvements in data manipulation and visualisation now allow firms to create genuinely useful 'dashboards' to help their people see how they and the firm are performing. One of the most notable law firms in this respect is DWF, whose technology platform brings together a wealth of hard financial data with softer measures such as client feedback and personal objectives.

Alongside better presentation of data, firms are also using increasingly sophisticated social tools. Blogs and similar platforms have been used for some years, but these are now just one part of a range of methods for people to communicate about and reflect on their work and interests. Platforms like HighQ's Collaborate product provide opportunities for people to create content in blogs and wikis, but can also publish information automatically in the form of a Twitter-like activity stream to show what work is being done.

Improvements in connectivity and openness will improve the flow of information around the firm so that opportunities for innovation are much more visible than before. They can also improve the quality of collaboration on ideas. Firms will only see these benefits if people adapt to them and use them as part of their normal workflow. Data dashboards are only useful if people act on what they see. Social platforms depend on genuine broad engagement; otherwise, they serve no purpose other than to amplify a few loud voices. Successful use of tools like these therefore depends on high levels of trust across the firm. The systems themselves need to be trustworthy, and people need to trust that the information they volunteer will not be misused by others. That kind of trust takes time to build if it isn't present already. Firms that already have high levels of trust will be able to develop their knowledge capability much faster as a consequence.

The prospect for knowledge capability and innovation in law firms

This account of the future may seem unattainable, even bleak. How can firms feel confident enough to move from traditional KM to a higher potential, but risky, knowledge capability approach? In fact, there are two key factors that may make it easier for law firms than for some other organisations to develop the right connectivity, openness, and trust to allow deeper knowledge capability to develop.

Unlike many commercial organisations, law firms tend to have a very clear focus. They help clients with the law. They don't often dilute that aim with services that are remote from the law, and the aim itself is well understood across the firm (not just by lawyers). Law firms also tend not to be very large. Very few contain more than 2–3,000 people. The combination of clarity of purpose and smallish size provides good conditions for trust to develop. With high levels of trust, better connectivity and openness facilitated by the right technical tools is more likely to be successful.

The second key factor for many law firms is the presence of professional support lawyers (PSLs) who can act as catalysts for optimum use of new tools and processes. While PSLs were initially recruited to take care of traditional KM activities, it would be a mistake to think that their role has stayed the same for the past 20–30 years. In fact, many PSLs already act as connectors between lawyers and other professionals across their firms. They stimulate the development of new products and services, and they often play important roles in teams making transformative changes in client service delivery and internal operations. In firms that have yet to make such changes, many PSLs are role models for the kind of trust and openness that firms need more widely. They also tend to be much more aware of the possibilities for change than many others in the firm.

Good innovation comes from a broad perspective on the world, an openness to novel insights and influences, reliable access to knowledge and insights across the firm (and from outside – clients and suppliers), and an organisational expectation that these should all come together coherently. That demands forward-looking knowledge activities, and PSLs are well placed to drive such work. Unlike their PSLs, most firms are only slowly waking up to the possibilities presented by a more forward-looking approach to understanding and developing their knowledge.

Whatever technologies or processes they choose, firms that actively pool and use the knowledge that all their people have – of their clients and their markets, of the legal market, of legal change on the horizon, and of the capabilities and limitations of the firm itself – are much more likely to be able to develop a coherent strategic response to the challenges they face. That response will inevitably be innovative, but it will also be impossible without the right knowledge capability.

About the author

Mark Gould is the founder of Mark Gould Consulting, a business focused on helping law firms use their knowledge more productively. He works with firms of all sizes, helping them to stand out in their markets by acting as a catalyst for improvement, combining his understanding of the legal sector with the firm's deep knowledge. He was head of knowledge management at Addleshaw Goddard LLP between 2006 and 2014, and a PSL at the same firm from 2001. Prior to that, he spent 13 years teaching law at the University of Bristol.

Chapter 4: The frameworks of strategic innovation

By Richard Hinwood, strategy and governance executive at Withers LLP

'There is nothing more difficult to take in hand, more perilous to conduct, or more uncertain in its success, than to take the lead in the introduction of a new order of things...'
Niccolò Machiavelli

Innovation – Two definitions:
i. The introduction of a new thing.
ii. The alteration of something established.
Oxford English Dictionary

Eureka!

Eureka! That unique, unbridled moment of happiness after making the next big discovery is often one of the first images to enter people's minds when they think about innovation. However, innovation is rarely something that happens overnight. Nor are the results of innovation necessarily as groundbreaking as those achieved by some of the most famous innovations in history, from the Universal Machine to the Dyson vacuum cleaner (which is definitely not a Hoover!). However, that doesn't mean that our own innovations can't still be incredibly valuable to our businesses.

In this chapter, I'll outline several different frameworks for strategic innovation. Each framework has a different purpose within the innovation programme. My intention is to leave you with the choice as to which of the frameworks might be the most useful to you. Each framework can be applied independently or in conjunction with any of the others. You may even combine several of the frameworks in a personally innovative way. I can't promise to lead you to Eureka! However, I will outline some of the frameworks that, at the very least, will provide a solid starting point for strategic innovation. Finding that Eureka! moment is then down to you.

Strategic innovation

Innovation is complex because it involves a range of disciplines – strategy, technology, people, projects, finance, change – all of which need to be co-ordinated. Any legal business can be innovative. The main challenge, especially for established legal businesses, is to understand *how* to become innovative. The frameworks outlined in this chapter should help you to answer each of the following questions:

- What are the main elements of strategic innovation? *The Pentathlon Framework*;
- How do we need to change to implement strategic innovation? *The Innovation Audit*;
- Does strategic innovation really apply to the provision of services? *Service Blueprinting*;
- How can we take advantage of existing strategic innovation solutions? *The Morphological Box*;
- How can strategic innovation lead to competitive advantage? *The Four Actions Framework*; and
- How can we lead strategic innovation effectively? *Tipping Point Leadership.*

The Pentathlon Framework – It's not just about the ideas...

The Pentathlon Framework[1] outlines the five key elements of strategic innovation management: innovation strategy, ideas, prioritisation, implementation, and people and organisation. It is a valuable starting point for understanding how to approach innovation in methodical and logical way.

Innovation strategy

The existence of an innovation strategy is central to the creation of long-term value through innovation. At its simplest, an innovation strategy needs to set out: how your innovation process will support your business's aims for growth; what mix of radical and incremental innovation you wish to include; and how the voice of your client will be built into the innovation process. Without a sufficiently clear and well-thought-through innovation strategy, there's less chance that any innovation you do undertake will be of benefit to your business.

Ideas, prioritisation, and implementation

The three elements in the middle of the pentathlon framework form the 'development funnel'.[2] The front end of the funnel is for your ideas. Individual thinking, group brainstorming, and various methods of research can all help to spark and generate ideas. Thinking and brainstorming is often best done away from computers. Ideally, you want any ideas generated to be 'focused ideas' – not perfectly formed yet, but focused on solving or answering a particular problem or challenge. This need can be taken directly from specific client feedback, from a similar need observed in a related sector, or even from general market research. As you'll see from the Morphological Box later on, a simple constraint, such as having to target ideas towards a neatly defined challenge, can actually encourage creativity rather than constrain it. In group brainstorming sessions, why not challenge the participants to present each of their ideas on just one post-it note – simplicity and clarity shouldn't be lost in creativity. Finally, don't kill any ideas just yet. However crazy or offbeat an initial idea may seem, the killing of ideas too early will also kill the creativity process.

The middle stage of the development funnel is for prioritisation. You won't want to pursue all of the ideas proposed at the front end of the funnel. Similarly, you may wish to pursue some ideas first, before others, or even to combine several ideas and progress them together. The prioritisation decision-making process needs to be effective, rational, and transparent. Ideally, it should also be relatively quick.

Different criteria should be applied depending on whether the innovation being sought is radical or incremental in nature. Assessment of incremental ideas should be closest to the way you assess the value of business cases. Although you won't have much detail to consider for any of the ideas, how closely it aligns to the challenge set, how realistically it can be achieved in the timescale you have, and how financially viable it is likely to be may all be useful criteria to consider. The extent and availability of your implementation resource should also be taken into account. The assessment criteria for radical innovation ideas should be different in one key way. Financial viability is a poor criterion to include for prioritising radical innovation ideas. Instead, greater weight could be assigned to the way in which each radical innovation idea would support your overall innovation strategy.

At the end of the prioritisation process, you should have an initial plan for which ideas to implement and in which order, with an indication of how much resource should be assigned to each implementation before it is further assessed, and a list of indicative criteria for what the implementation needs to prove or achieve for it to be worth continuing to allocate further resource to each of the prioritised ideas.

The final stage of the development funnel concerns implementation. Successful implementation of any idea will almost invariably require some degree of resource – time, energy, and money. As a result, it's important that you only implement ideas that have the potential to benefit your business. You do not have to fully implement all of the ideas that you prioritised. It may only be through partial implementation that you discover the true potential (or lack of it!) of an idea that at least looked good in theory. Implementation is certainly not a one-stage process. A balance needs to be stuck between reviewing the likely end value of each prioritised idea as you implement it (which should become clearer the further you get towards final implementation) and keeping the number of review stages to a minimum in order to reduce the overall administrative burden of allocating further resource for each stage of the implementation process. The decision to go or kill is just as much a part of implementation as of prioritisation. Choosing to kill an idea as soon as you realise that it no longer has the potential to benefit your firm is not only good practice, but also crucial to the success of your innovation programme, not least because it protects your valuable resources and enables you to reassign them to other initiatives.

Hopefully, at least some of the ideas that you prioritised and implemented will be developed to the point that they can be introduced to your clients. Involving some of your clients throughout the development process should help to ensure that the final implementation of your innovation work is as valuable to them as possible. Similarly, involving your legal staff and business development professionals in the process will help to minimise the gap between what you say you can provide and what you can *actually* provide.

People and organisation

While successful implementation may lead to a Eureka! moment for a given idea, it does not guarantee that your overall innovation programme will be as successful as you would like it to be. To achieve this, you also have to focus on the role that your people and your organisation play in creating and supporting a culture of innovation. Some people within your organisation will be more engaged with your innovation programme than others. Promote the value of creativity and provide the time and physical space for that to occur. Encourage cross-functional and cross-office collaboration to share challenges and propose ideas to solve them. Empower and support those who are willing to engage with innovation. Ask them about their experiences of working on innovation within your firm – what hurdles do they encounter, how do they overcome these (or what prevents them overcoming them), and who else do they rely on to succeed in driving your innovation programme forward. You may not have all of the answers to the hurdles that they face, but as you'll see in Tipping Point Leadership, there's still a lot that you can do to help them to overcome these and achieve success. Finally, including innovation criteria in formal assessments can also be beneficial in ensuring that your reward systems align with your corporate-level strategy and the behaviour that you want to see in order to achieve this.

Why a pentathlon?

Just as with the sporting pentathlon, successful management of strategic innovation requires strong performance in all five areas. If any one area is weak or missing, overall success is far less likely. Similarly, excellence in just one or two areas will not lead to competitive advantage. The next section, 'The innovation audit', will show you how to put the pentathlon framework into action.

The Innovation Audit

The concept of Innovation Audits first appeared in the 1980s. They were originally focused solely on creativity, but can now be used to determine the level of current innovation performance within a business. Innovation Audits are generally qualitative in nature (there are few reliable quantitative measures of innovation performance) and are usually conducted through a questionnaire format. There are many different ways to structure an Innovation Audit, but to be effective the audit has to cover all areas of innovation management. The following proposed Innovation Audit questions are based around each of the areas of the Pentathlon Framework[3] – you will invariably want to expand on this list:

- Is innovation stated as part of your firm strategy and business plans?
- Do you regularly review your portfolio of services from an innovation perspective?
- Do you have clear and stated objectives for your innovation program to achieve?
- Do you have an ongoing process for people to generate and contribute new ideas?
- Do you actively consider how new technologies can be applied to your business?
- Do you have a clear and effective process for prioritising ideas?
- Does your financial reporting system reflect innovation as an investment or a cost?
- Do you support staff who try out new ideas, even if their ideas fail?
- Do you provide training for staff in innovation-related skills?

Ideally, you should invite employees from right across your firm to complete the questionnaire. It's not uncommon for different levels of the organisation to respond very differently to the Innovation Audit. This will immediately provide you with insight into the gaps in your innovation process and areas to focus on improving. Hopefully, it will also highlight areas of strength that you can maintain, build on, and learn from. Is it really possible to be innovative in service provision, rather than just through products? The next section, Service Blueprinting, will provide you with an effective starting point to do just that.

Service Blueprinting

When you consider the nature of services, it's no wonder that most innovation is focused on products. Even at their best, services are intangible, variable, and delivered over both time and space. As a result, we often attempt to describe services by words alone, but this in turn leads to over-simplification, incompleteness, and a lack of differentiation. However, all is not lost. The Service Blueprint is a simple yet powerful framework to include in your innovation process.

The Service Blueprint[4] is a framework that helps to connect four different aspects of service provision – the value of the service (what your client is willing to pay for), the form and function of the service (the key steps in delivery), the nature of the service experience (the key steps in which the experience occurs), and the service outcomes (the tangible and intangible outcomes). The service blueprint is effectively a flow diagram highlighting the critical interactions between your firm and your clients. To start, you first have to analyse the initial actions of the client. How do they:

- First hear of your firm;
- Research your firm;
- First contact your firm;
- Stay in contact with your firm; and
- Provide feedback to your firm?

From there, you move in turn to their interactions with the visible members of your firm (including your secretaries, lawyers, and receptionists). Next, add in the interactions between the visible members of your firm and your invisible members (including your client research team, business development team, and knowledge management team), as well as the processes that they use to help create the end value for your clients. Finally, also add in the physical evidence aspects of your service that also shape your clients' experience of dealing with your firm (your website, offices, documentation, and the appearance of your staff).

The completed Service Blueprint is unlikely to include anything that you didn't already know. However, it includes three important features. First, it is created from the basis of putting the client first and working from their actions, rather than starting with the firm. Secondly, the Service Blueprint highlights the temporal element of service provision, which is something that you need to provide consistency across in order to achieve the desired client experience. Finally, the process of creating the Service Blueprint as well as the flow diagram itself will invariably lead to the generation of ideas as to how and where to improve your client experience. Ideas? You've now already found one clear way to get into the development funnel of the Pentathlon Framework. The next section, The Morphological Box, will show you another way into the innovation process.

The Morphological Box

As highlighted by the definitions at the start of this chapter, innovation can mean doing something totally new, but it can also involve creating a new combination of attributes that already exist in several different other models. The Morphological Box is an effective way of identifying the key attributes you should focus on in your own innovation process. It's also a good example of how structure can drive creativity.

The Morphological Box was derived from the work of Fritz Zwicky, a Swiss physicist at the Institute of Technology in California in the 1930s. The simplest form of Morphological Box can be set out in a table. Each column consists of an existing model/solution that you have identified as relevant to the area of innovation you are looking to undertake. On each of the rows, list the various attributes that combine to make up the overall service (examples of attributes could include level of partner involvement, depth of client relationship management, degree of tailoring, degree of outsourcing, and pricing methodology). Each attribute will have different parameters. For example, level of partner involvement could range from always having two or more partners working on a matter, to always having one partner involved, but only for sign off, down to partner involvement only on the largest of matters. You then complete the table by assigning the relevant parameter of each attribute to the difference models listed in each column. Most existing models will differ from one another on one or more of the attributes.

As we already know, different business models work for different businesses. Once you've completed the table, you can then choose the most desirable parameter for each attribute for your innovation, and circle each one in the table. The chances are that your desired attribute parameter list will involve a pick and mix of attributes from across at least two of the different models you included in your table. This new configuration will give you a potentially unique innovation compared to the competition. As Arthur Schopenhauer once said, 'The task is not so much to see what no one has yet seen, but to think what nobody has yet thought about that which everyone sees.'

The following section, The Four Actions Framework, can help you to take the Morphological Box framework one step further.

The Four Actions Framework

The Four Actions Framework is one of several frameworks included in Kim & Mauborgne's

Blue Ocean Strategy.[5] At its core, Blue Ocean Strategy is about value innovation – *increasing* the value that you provide to your clients while *decreasing* your cost of providing this service. The Four Actions Framework involves asking four questions that can help to redefine how and where your firm adds value. The four questions are:

- What are the basic elements of the legal sector that most firms take for granted, but don't actually add any value to your clients?
- What are the basic elements that are a necessity of the legal sector, but fail to differentiate your firm from your competitors?
- What are the basic elements of the legal sector that add value to your clients, that you excel in, and that differentiate your firm from your competitors?
- What elements that are not traditionally part of the legal sector can you introduce to your service that will add additional value to your clients?

The appropriate actions you should take in response to your answers for each of the four questions above are:

- *Eliminate* any basic factors that don't add value;
- *Reduce* any basic elements that don't differentiate you;
- *Increase* any basic elements that add value, you excel in, and differentiate you; and
- *Create* new elements that will add even greater value to your clients.

Combining the Four Actions Framework with the Morphological Box will potentially give you a uniquely valuable solution. That's not to say that the 'eliminate, reduce, increase, create' process leads to decisions that are clear, straightforward, and easy to implement. As with the implementation of all innovations, effective leadership is crucial. The next section, Tipping Point Leadership, provides a powerful framework that can be utilised even in the face of the most difficult hurdles to overcome.

Tipping Point Leadership

Tipping Point Leadership is a leadership approach that is focused on bringing about fundamental change quickly, despite limited resources.[6] Perhaps the best example of this leadership approach in action concerns the work of Bill Bratton, who as the police commissioner of the New York Police Department from 1994 to 1996 transformed the city from a crime-ridden 'rotten apple' into the safest city in the US. He achieved this transformation in less than two years, with no increase in budget, despite the fact that the NYPD was notoriously difficult to manage. How did he achieve this? By focusing on overcoming four key hurdles: cognitive, resource, motivational, and political. Perhaps more importantly, how can *you* use this approach to achieve fundamental change through your innovation programmes?

1. Cognitive hurdle

In order to make a compelling case for change, ensure that senior management experience first hand the problems faced by those in your firm who support your innovation programme.

Example: New Yorkers considered the subway to be one of the most dangerous places in the city. However, it wasn't an area of focus for the police. Bratton required all police officers to ride the subway to work. They soon changed their minds – the subway had to become a priority.

The employees who most believe in your innovation programme should readily tell you the biggest challenges that they face. Your challenge is to help senior management put themselves in the position to experience these problems themselves and come to the same understanding that you have as to why these issues have to be addressed.

2. Resource hurdle

If you have limited resources, what are your options? Reduce your aspirations? Should you do so, you'll fail to achieve as much through your innovation programme as you could. Fight for greater resource? The risk of doing so is that you'll divert attention from the real underlying problems. Instead, why not take the bold decision to concentrate your resource on the area(s) most urgently in need of change?

Example: The majority of crimes happened at a select number of stations – Bratton focused his manpower there rather than splitting it across all of the subway network.

If you can identify the greatest challenges to the overall success of your innovation programme, you already know where you need to target your resource. In doing so, you may leave other areas under-resourced. In the short term, that's not a problem. If you fail to overcome the most significant challenges, the lack of resource will continue to be a growing problem. However, target it on the area(s) most in need of change and you'll generate the real potential to create fundamental change.

3. Motivational hurdle

Not everyone in your firm will want to believe in, participate in, or even see the success of your innovation programme. Perhaps surprisingly, *that doesn't matter.* What matters is influencing key individuals who in turn can create the momentum necessary for fundamental change.

Example: Precinct commanders were the key influencers in the NYPD. Bratton put them under the spotlight, grilled every other week by their superiors and their juniors. The result? A culture of performance, accountability, and learning.

Who is it in your firm that carries the greatest influencing power? Do they already believe in your innovation programme? If so, you've got a perfect start. If not, what do you need to do to bring them on board? Is this somewhere that you have to focus you resource early on in order to make a fundamental change? While people can often be a barrier to change, people are also the greatest drivers of change. Make sure that the most influential people in your business have a vested interested in supporting the success of your innovation programme.

4. Political hurdle

Even as you approach the tipping point of change, powerful vested interests can still act to undermine a fundamental shift. What's the best way to identify and manage the key doubters in your business? Ensure that a respected senior member of the firm plays a key part in your innovation programme.

Example: Bratton appointed a veteran police officer, Timoney, as his second in command. Timoney knew the key individuals and personalities within NYPD far better than Bratton – he'd worked for the NYPD for over 20 years. He made sure that Bratton was not undermined by the most dangerous of saboteurs.

This is arguably the toughest of the hurdles to overcome. As a result, it's also one worth focusing on – you can't afford to ignore this threat. As Machiavellian as it may sound, you responsibility to your firm and your firm's innovation programme is to isolate any negative voices. There are likely to be a range of reasons why different parties within your firm should support – if not actively promote or participate in – your innovation programme. Take the time to speak with each of these parties and strengthen and grow the potential areas of mutual interest. If you do this, you won't be the only person who has a vested interest in ensuring the success of your firm's innovation programme.

Conclusion

Successfully integrating strategic innovation into a legal business is without doubt a significant challenge. Importantly, it's also an achievable goal to set and a rewarding goal to accomplish. It's not just about ideas and creativity, it's more like a pentathlon. It's important to know where you are starting from as well as where you want to get to. You can achieve innovation through services, take advantage of existing innovations, and achieve competitive advantage through strategic innovation, all with limited resources. Some legal businesses, as you'll see later in this report, are already doing this. The only question left is, will you do so too?

About the author

Richard Hinwood is the strategy and governance executive at Withers LLP, where he focuses on the formulation and implementation of the firm's key strategic initiatives. Richard is a qualified solicitor and holds an MBA from Cranfield School of Management. Key areas of personal focus include: strategic innovation, international strategy, new venture creation, organisational behaviour, and implementing change. Richard can be contacted by email at: richard.hinwood@withersworldwide.com and on LinkedIn at https://uk.linkedin.com/in/richardhinwood.

References

1. Goffin, K. & Mitchell, R., *Innovation Management: Strategy and Implementation Using the Pentathlon Framework*, 2nd Edition, Palgrave Macmillan, Basingstoke, 2010.
2. Majaro, S., *The Creative Gap*, Longman, London,1988.
3. Based on Anonymous, 'Managing Change in Your Organization', *International Trade Forum*, No. 2, 2000, pp. 26–28.
4. Bitner, M.J., Ostrom, A.L., and Morgan, F.N., 'Service Blueprinting: A Practical Technique for Service Innovation', *California Management Review*, vol. 50, no. 3 (Spring 2008), pp.66–94.
5. Kim, W.C., Mauborgne, R., *Blue Ocean Strategy: How to Create Uncontested Market Space and Make the Competition Irrelevant*, Harvard Business School Press, Boston, 2005.
6. Ibid.

Chapter 5: Rethinking pricing – Why fixed fees and value pricing are not pricing innovations

By Chris Howe, director of Raedbora Consulting

PRICING IN the legal industry has long been dominated by the use of the hourly rate. While lawyers were in demand and firms simply had to throw open their doors for work to flood in, this was fine. No great thought was required to set pricing – one simply referred to the firm's published rate card and calculated the fee. Clients effectively had no choice if they wanted to get the work done. Lawyers undoubtedly missed opportunities to charge premiums when clients got the benefit of years of experience in a few minutes' advice, which saved them large sums. But, in general, lawyers were the main beneficiaries with high profit levels coupled with very limited commercial risk as clients were effectively paying 'cost plus'.

This landscape has of course completely changed since the economic downturn, creating significant challenges for some firms, but also opportunities. Clients are using the change in the balance of power to shift the balance of risk too. This is likely to be a permanent change in the legal landscape and it requires innovative approaches to both the client relationship and pricing.

Under the pre-recession pricing model, lawyers took virtually no commercial risk, expecting the client to take the impact of all unexpected events. These can range from bad estimating through to ineffective or inefficient work. Also, external events can throw a project off track through no fault of either the client or lawyer. The only risk sitting with the lawyer was the risk arising from poor advice.

There are plenty of examples of client frustration with the overall commercial service provided by lawyers. In one notable example, a client gave the following feedback: 'You quoted 100K for the job. There was no further discussion about fees until the bill arrived. When that showed a bill of 400K, you made me look like an idiot, as I had to go back to the board for authorisation for the extra money after the event.'

This illustrates a number of points:

- Lawyers need to be good project managers as well as legal experts, which includes tracking progress and reporting changes early;
- Lawyers must understand how their clients work and adapt to it. In this case, the manager had obtained authorisation only for the fees estimated;
- There is an assumption that the client will take all overruns. If you are seeking to align your interests with those of your clients and build long term relationships, consider if this is sustainable; and
- Unexpected changes either by the client or third parties are no excuse for slack management of a project or fees.

In this case, the legal team had done a fantastic job in trying circumstances – but was the client satisfied? Clearly not.

What is innovation?

Client surveys are increasingly showing that

pricing is, contrary to what we may all have thought, not in their top five concerns. Value for money, however, is. Clients of course increasingly ask lawyers about innovative pricing – and indeed it has become almost de rigeur to include such a question in panel reviews. But, there is no point in innovation for innovation's sake – it does not necessarily align you with your client's interests.

One bidding team responded to a question about innovative pricing with a striking and bold offer, which while containing some considerable commercial risk offered big opportunities for both the client and the law firm. The response received was 'in the nicest possible way, you've called our bluff on "innovative" pricing'. The offer was too innovative for the client to digest, but it did demonstrate the team's ability to think outside the box, and was viewed favourably.

Innovation is 'the development of new value through solutions that meet new needs, or adding value to old customers by providing new ways of maximising their current level of productivity… Innovation differs from invention in that innovation refers to the use of a better and, as a result, novel idea or method, whereas invention refers more directly to the creation of the idea or method itself. Innovation differs from improvement in that innovation refers to the notion of doing something different rather than doing the same thing better.'[1]

When developing innovative pricing methods, you should look first to solutions that meet your clients' needs more effectively. You do not have to create these methods from scratch, but simply use approaches you find elsewhere – perhaps in other industries. Proper understanding of your client is critical. Conversely, simply reducing your prices is not innovative.

Critical to the successful development of innovative pricing is a different mode of thinking by lawyers. This means losing many of the assumptions that dominate their thinking when it comes to pricing. Below are some good principles to follow:

- Clearly separate price from cost – Using hourly rate cards to price will lead to bad decisions and lost business. The hourly rate includes assumptions about levels of overhead and profit that simply do not reflect the true workings of the law firm business model.
- Understand the competitive environment – Price should be based on what the output is worth, which in turn should be based on the market rate for that output.
- Know what is profitable – Assuming that you cannot do the work 'because it isn't profitable' may lose good business. I have yet to meet a lawyer who, when challenged, could demonstrate how he knew a particular price level was unprofitable.
- Don't race to the bottom – Clients don't necessarily want the cheapest price. Some do, but in many instances a 'good' price that the supplier can stick to is far preferable for planning purposes.
- Know the meaning of 'quality' – To many lawyers, this means the best job possible. To many clients, this means reliability, consistency, and repeatability.

Pricing innovation myths

Let's now look at a couple of pricing approaches and consider whether they really are innovative, then identify the key elements of real innovation.

Fixed fees

This is the solution most commonly offered as the alternative to hourly rates. In its favour, it is already widely used, with a number of large and small law firms doing the majority of their work on this basis. The key benefits are that:

- It is simple and easily understood by both the client and lawyer;

- There is no requirement for detailed tracking of time – if the job is done, the bill is known; and
- Some key risks are passed to the lawyer (including the lawyer's own inefficiencies).

However, there are disadvantages, which include that:

- It is inflexible when things change – leaving either party potentially out of pocket; and
- There is pressure on lawyers to compromise quality by using underqualified resources.

In many cases, true fixed fees are not actually used, as lawyers agree to bill 'what is on the clock' if the matter finishes early. This means that it is not really a fixed fee at all, but more akin to a capped fee. Arguably, the lawyer loses both ways, being unable to earn extra profit if costs are less than expected, but also being still stuck with the fixed fee if the matter overruns.

Value pricing

There is much discussion about value pricing as a way forward. The idea is that the price is determined by the value of the output delivered, rather than the work done. In principle, this seems very attractive as it means the lawyer is able to extract a price related to the difference his work has made to the client, and it appears to play to clients' requests for 'value for money'. Many are promoting this approach as the means of resolving the pricing dilemma and have developed some complicated 'solutions'.

However, pricing has to exist in the real work. Value pricing has a number of flaws in this context:

- It misrepresents clients' true requirements – When clients look for 'value for money', this does not mean that they want to pay lawyers the full value created by their input; it means they wish to maximise the net value achieved for their shareholders. Clients will not necessarily go for the cheapest option, but the one that leaves the most net value with them after paying their lawyers' bills.
- It ignores the true competitive environment – When in competition with other providers, a value-based solution risks seriously either under- or over-pricing the solution. Clients are unlikely to choose a higher price just because it is innovative.
- Measurement of value is difficult – Sometimes there can be significant effort to robustly establish the value added. For example, one competing firm actually spent more time on determining, agreeing, and measuring the pricing metrics than on doing the work.

One key positive of value pricing is that it is making law firms separate price from cost.

Real pricing innovation

So, what does constitute innovative pricing – and how do you achieve it? The key elements of an innovative pricing solution are:

- Proper understanding of the client's requirements and your firm's requirements, translated into the commercial agreement between the parties;
- Value for money in all outcomes, taking into account appropriate reward for risks taken;
- A clear and simple approach that is easily understood; and
- A model that takes account of the competition, their capabilities, and their competing prices.

Finally, any pricing decision should then test whether the work can be done profitably and, more particularly, how the work can be organised to maximise profits.

Clearly, each truly innovative

arrangement will be specific to the parties involved and the circumstances of the deal. The terms are frequently confidential and it isn't easy to describe them, even after redacting names, without disclosing intellectual capital. Below are a couple of examples that are already in the public domain that illustrate the key principles.

Case study 1: Pfizer

Anyone interested in innovative pricing in the legal sector would do well to learn about Pfizer's panel arrangements. In general terms, a series of law firms have been invited onto this panel. In return for a 'guaranteed' fee, they are required to cooperate with each other and to take on whatever work Pfizer requires of them. This is innovative not only because there is no direct relationship between the work done and the fee, but also because much of the administration of the supplier relationship is swept away.

There are some key points to note here:

- While the arrangement seems alien to the legal market, it is quite common in engineering supply and servicing arrangements (see, for example, the UK's rail industry);
- The change was clearly driven by the GC of Pfizer and law firms either took part or left the panel;
- Much of the admin and conflict over billing was swept away;
- Law firms have a mutual interest in cooperation; and
- The arrangement not only promotes but is dependent upon long-term working relationships, so it will be difficult for new firms to enter the panel.

This is a clear example of a client using the panel arrangement to re-engineer the supply of legal services. This was only possible because of the buying power that the client was able to exert – but this is also the case for many clients.

This type of arrangement is becoming more prevalent and clients are actively considering similar arrangements right now. Law firms must be able to proactively deal with such challenges by properly understanding the services and cost of services provided to clients and be able to manage the client relationship effectively if they are to take part. Those who are unable to take part – or choose not to – can expect to be locked out of panels for prolonged periods of time.

Case study 2: CMS Cameron McKenna

CMS Cameron McKenna's report 'The Future of Fees' lists a number of different pricing methods that are worth considering. One that is worthy of note is the idea of accepting payment in barrels of oil from a client. This is innovative because it transfers the risk of oil price movement from the client to the law firm – presumably this reduces risk for the client because it deals in oil. It also shows that the firm has clearly understood one of the main constraints for the client to proceed with the work and has sought to alleviate it.

However, this is really an innovative funding arrangement rather than innovative pricing, as it simply addresses the method of payment. It is also a risky arrangement, as law firms do not generally have any expertise in or methods of managing oil price risk. A better risk transfer would be one where a risk that the client cannot control is moved to the law firm which can control it.

Test your firm's ability to generate innovative pricing models

Which pricing model is most common in your business?

Type	Points
Hourly rates	5
Fixed fees	15
Conditional fee arrangements	20
Flexible models	20

Comment: Step one in innovative pricing is ensuring you know which options you already have. The lowest score is for hourly rates, as these are not innovative. Fixed fees are a quick fix and may be appropriate in some cases, especially retail, but are quite inflexible.

How do you decide your pricing?

Type	Points
Individual partners	5
Client teams of partners	10
Business support role	15

Comment: Key to good innovative pricing is the old adage 'two heads are better than one'. The best results of all will be obtained by involving those with different experiences and perspectives, so draw on the accounts and business developers in your business.

Do you track your pricing success and failures?

Type	Points
No	0
Yes – within teams	10
Yes – across the business	25

Comment: After all the analysis, there will still be an element of trial and error, and much can be learned from prior successful and unsuccessful bids. You need to track these.

Total score

0–25 points: Plenty of work to do. You may be hitting on the odd innovative method, but it might be hard to deliver innovation consistently.

25–50 points: The groundwork is there, but you need to make better use of the experience you have in the business.

50+ points: You have the wherewithal to deliver innovative solutions.

Different perspectives

What these case studies demonstrate is the need to understand the situation as viewed by both the client and law firm and, importantly, how the risks and concerns in that situation can be translated into a hard pricing agreement.

However, it seems that law firms are still behind their clients on this issue, as is demonstrated by the Pfizer example. Clearly, without change from law firms, clients can and will impose that change.

A version of this article first appeared in Managing Partner *magazine in April 2013.*

About the author

Chris Howe is a director of Raedbora Consulting and advises legal clients on pricing, practice management (including restructuring and day-to-day performance improvement), and the operational aspects of mergers. He also advises buyers of legal services on legal procurement reviews.

Chris's clients include top 20 international law firms as well as FTSE 100 businesses. For ten years he was divisional director and commercial director of a UK top 20 law firm where he was head of pricing and conducted innovative research into pricing with Cranfield School of Management. He also has ten years' consulting experience with PwC, Ernst & Young, and Deloitte.

Chris is an international speaker and author on pricing and professional services.

Reference

1. www.en.wikipedia.org/wiki/innovation.

Chapter 6: Innovations in legal technology

By Toby Brown, chief practice officer at Akin Gump

WITH INCREASED pressures on law firms to do more for less, many firms have abandoned the billable hour for more innovative pricing structures. What is missing is a technology that will allow lawyers to track the profitability of these new deals. This is the next logical innovation in law firms, but it is not as straightforward as it sounds. This article discusses how such a system would operate, and the barriers that must be removed from the road in order for it to succeed.

At the recent conference on cutting edge legal technology innovations, the topics under discussion were bold: big data, document automation, computational law. Yet, as one conference delegate tweeted, much of the technology that is already available is hardly being used by lawyers. As we explore technological innovations in the legal market, we will be wise to maintain our grip on this reality. It may be much more interesting to prognosticate ahead and explore the limitless possibilities as to how technology may be able to transform the practice of law. However, in the real world, many lawyers struggle to use existing or even dated technologies (e.g. document generation).

At the same conference, lawyer-turned-entrepreneur Casey Flaherty tweeted, 'I am out there trying to get them to use Word (est 1983) semi-well'. Casey Flaherty is well known for his outside counsel test on using basic functions in Word and Excel. Let's just say the lawyers who take this test don't score well. Implementing IBM's Watson technology at a firm might be a quantum jump, but it is probably not the next step in technology for lawyers. So, what is the next step? Or better yet, what should it be? One thing that is essential – as the dismal results of Flaherty's Legal Tech Audit show – is that lawyers won't use this technology unless there is a compelling need for them to do so.

Contrary to what many might suggest, in my view, finding ways for technology to make information more accessible for partners is the next, best step, rather than looking for transformative technology. A prime target for this is technology focused on accessing financial information and presenting it in an easily digestible, usable fashion.

Untapped data

At present, most lawyers do not use, or sparingly use, the financial systems at law firms. This has been the case for three main reasons:

- First, lawyers in the past did not care that much about this information. Partners at firms were getting rich without having to care much about the financial details surrounding their business. Rates were going up faster than associate compensation, and billable hours were plentiful. This situation has obviously changed. Now there is a growing hunger to have actionable access to this information.
- Second, as a result of lawyers not wanting immediate access to financial

information, these legacy financial systems were built with accounting functions in mind. Therefore, the user interfaces resemble spreadsheets. Rows upon rows and columns following columns of information are presented. For those in finance and accounting roles, this is a comfortable and useful approach. These people want to see *all* of the detail so they can understand all of the potential financial drivers for a given matter or client. Presenting this spreadsheet style data on clients to lawyers, however, rarely goes over well.

- Finally, firms have been hesitant about sharing this information too broadly – at least in an easily accessible way.

As concerns the first point above, this situation has obviously changed in recent years. Law firms today are more concerned with maximising profits, clients are more demanding about how their work is performed and more prepared to question the bill, and with this has come a growing hunger for real-time financial information that will help lawyers to work more efficiently and effectively.

It is true, as I have said, that lawyers are not ready adopters of new technology; theirs is a profession steeped in tradition and they tend to work from a view point of 'if it ain't broke, don't fix it'. But lawyers are not adverse to innovation. Take, for example, 'alternative fee arrangements', which are now more broadly called 'pricing'. Lawyers have embraced considerable change in how they price their services. The point here is that change was not optional. The economic environment changed and created a need that begged for a technology solution. Compare this, for example, to CRM systems: CRM for years was pitched as a powerful tool for lawyers to grow their practices by understanding the known relationships across a firm. In reality, lawyers rarely leveraged those systems in that fashion because there was no pressing need to do so.

Now, I would argue – on the back of pricing innovations – lawyers have a real and compelling need to track the numbers for the pricing deals they have implemented. And this has grown into a more general need to track client and matter fees. These needs present a clear opportunity to innovate.

This brings us back to the proposed technology innovation. What is necessary, in my view, is to develop a technology that presents financial information in a simple, actionable, and transparent manner. In some respects, this innovation is focused on user interface or more accurately user experience. Instead of presenting volumes of data in spreadsheet views, it will present it in simple bar graphs with an option to drill into detail. Sounds easy, right? Not so much. Elegant technology is rarely easy. And that's what we are talking about here. In the case of law firms, there are a number of barriers to the implementation of such a system, and these are primarily related to the second two points above: the way in which law firm financial systems are built, which does not lend itself to the kind of technology I am describing; and the culture of many law firms, which dictates that information is shared on a strictly 'need to know' basis.

Moving beyond spreadsheets

Imagine trying to make the leap from DOS to iOS. Law firm financial information is not well structured for such a leap. Data practices in time and billing systems were not designed with such a purpose in mind. Tracking profitability at most firms was only done at very high levels. And like many technologies, time and billing is technology focused on collecting information for a primary purpose: generating invoices. This is not a criticism of the current crop of time and billing software systems; they function quite well for their intended purposes. It's just that the kind of reporting we are discussing was not on the list. If you look at how profitability is extracted and presented from these systems, it is typically done with another piece of software. True, with decent SQL query skills, you can manually pull all kinds of information – which is of coursed viewed in spreadsheets.

Most current financial reporting at law firms occurs in very manual ways. If a partner wants to see the numbers from a client or matter, a request is made to the accounting or financial group. This group may have a pre-built report that answers the partner's question, or they may have to manually extract the information with a new query. Whatever the approach, the partner receives a spreadsheet or table of information with the requested data. Especially when the data comes in a pre-built report, it likely comes with a lot of other data. These reports can be daunting, even to the accounting people. In order to fully understand what you are viewing, you need to have specific knowledge and experience, which most partners do not possess. Moreover, the request can take a day or two before a response is received. In my experience, these types of approaches lead to partners cherry-picking the data points that suit their situation and agenda. In fact, the numbers may not be good, but as long as the partner sees the data point of concern looking good, no further effort is made.

There are some firms now that provide summary data directly to their partners via dashboards or something similar. These dashboards provide high-level summaries of client and matter fee status, and some even provide profitability. This is obviously a step in the right direction, but merely providing information without functionality is of only limited use. For one thing, since it is usually only summary information, if there is any sort of question or concern about the numbers, the partners are straight back to the old method of calling accounting and requesting some detailed report.

The truth is that what partners need to see is relatively simple: is their work profitable? From there, they need to see why it looks good or not. Again, basic numbers present the answers along the lines of realisation and leverage. As noted above, those numbers actually do not exist in the time and billing systems. If a firm has a traditional profitability tool, it can calculate those stats. What is needed is simply the technology to draw out that information and present it in a more user-friendly fashion than a spread sheet.

Tackling transparency

The second barrier concerns transparent access to information. Partners are owners of their cases and have the right to see numbers relating to them, and so they will probably have full access to any financial system. As I have said, some firms are already presenting data directly to partners via dashboards etc., but many firms will be cautious about how far such sharing should go.

In the past, firms have resisted sharing financial information except on a strict 'need to know' basis. The main concern of firm leadership has been misinterpretation of the information, and possibly misuse. With most firms' current systems, misinterpretation is a risk because the information is so complex looking. It is easy for lawyers to come to conclusions the data may not truly support. Misuse comes about most often in relation to compensation. Partners only see the numbers that support an increase in their compensation and launch into lawyer-like arguments on why their compensation needs to be increased.

The next step

Ultimately, there are two core reasons why innovations in financial reporting stand a good chance of being adopted by law firms. First, the technology innovation needed is not anything on the cutting edge in terms of functionality. Instead, what is needed is modernised user interfaces and vastly improved user experiences. If you want lawyers to adopt technology, you will need to make it as usable as any app on their smartphones. If they have to go to a training course on how to use any technology, it will be DOA.

In the past, during internal presentations, I have asked the partners attending how many training sessions they have been to over the past year. 'None' is the most common answer. Even though they might benefit from the training, partners have limited time to spend on non-billable tasks. This precious time is better devoted to client development. So, innovative technology in this sense is technology that is intuitive and easy to use.

The second key point here is that technology that presents financial information is *important*. If a firm has a choice on where to apply more modern user interfaces, doing it on financial systems makes the most sense. This is information partners want and need. Over the past five or so years, the need for financial information has slowly grown. We are now at the point where, in order to serve their clients well, lawyers need immediate and actionable access to this information. A user-friendly, relatively intuitive application that provides lawyers with access to financial information has a stronger chance at being adopted and utilised.

Innovation with impact?

It is always fun to focus on cutting-edge technology that presents opportunities for fundamental change. But if those technologies will not be adopted by lawyers, and especially partners, they can have little impact on the business of the firm.

Case study: Prosperoware's Umbria software

Many technology vendors are focusing on how to address this need for lawyers to access financial information more readily – both on the user interface (UI) side and with financial systems. One vendor that made a considerable leap in this arena is Prosperoware with their Umbria system. Umbria provides real-time profitably information on the matter and client level. This allows lawyers to have the immediate access they are craving. When a client calls on the 20th and inquires about the month's fee status, the lawyer can quickly answer the question, without calling the accounting department or having someone else access the information. Being able to quickly respond to client questions about fees brings tremendous value to the lawyers' finger tips.

Feedback so far from lawyers using this system almost always includes very favourable comments. In one instance, a partner had an extra monitor installed in his office just for viewing the application. In real-world application, Umbria seems to be hitting the mark.

What Umbria has accomplished of course sounds easy. It was not. In order to provide this type of solution, volumes of data are needed, along with the ability to calculate profitability metrics and present them in a simple fashion. When building such a system, it is very easy to be pulled in a direction of adding complexity. Lawyers are well known for asking for just one more feature that will make the application perfect for their use. This inevitably leads to an application with too much happening on the interface and features that do not get used in practice.

Umbria actually has very detailed information, down to the time entry level. But, again, the power of the tool comes not from an overwhelming presentation of detail, but instead from simple presentations at the right time and place in the application.

Umbria presents a great opportunity for firms to actually get partners to adopt technology. Hopefully, more providers will follow this example and move in this direction.

My advice to those living on the business side of law firms is to focus on technology innovations that will impact the bottom line. Look for technology connected closely to the profitability of a firm. The closer you are to the money, the bigger the impact you will have on a firm. Change will come when the business needs it. Without actionable access to the bottom line, lawyers will never focus on truly changing the business and embracing technology in a broader sense. So, even if the approach described in this article is not pushing 'sexy' technology, it will set the stage for that in the future.

About the author

Toby Brown is the chief practice officer (and was previously the director of strategic pricing & analytics) for Akin Gump (www.akingump.com). In this role, Toby works to develop creative pricing arrangements focused on meeting clients' needs. Also, in this role, he works with practice group leadership to identify and implement various efficiency-producing programmes and projects, including legal project management, process improvement, practice innovation, alternative staffing, and strategic partnering.

Prior to joining Akin Gump, Toby served in similar pricing roles for both Vinson & Elkins and Fulbright & Jaworski, where he also drove knowledge management (KM) initiatives and various marketing efforts. Previously, Toby served as a director for the Utah State Bar, operating various departments, including Communications, Technology, Continuing Legal Education, Access to Justice, and the Pro Bono Project.

Toby presents nationally on legal pricing, law practice management, financial management, knowledge management, legal marketing and business development, alternative fee arrangements, social media marketing, and other legal market subjects. He has also published numerous articles on these topics. Toby has served on a number of legal services boards, bar association task forces, and legal market organisations. He received the Peer Excellence Award, the President's Award, and the Anne Charles Award from the National Association of Bar Executives. He maintains the ABA-award-winning *3 Geeks and a Law Blog* with two colleagues at www.geeklawblog.com.

PART TWO

Case studies

Case study 1: Baker & McKenzie – Innovation in HR

Baker & McKenzie's innovative approach to personnel management has seen the global firm widely recognised as a leading employer in the legal industry. The following article outlines the initiatives that have helped create an environment that fosters professional and personal growth and engagement with the firm, and the steps the firm is taking to ensure its people continue to drive its agenda.

BAKER & McKenzie is well known as the original global law firm. It was founded in Chicago in the late 1940s, entered Latin America and Europe in the 1950s, Asia and Australia in the 1960s, and recently celebrated its 50th anniversary in London. With 11,000 people across nearly 80 offices worldwide, it is one of the largest law firms in the world. As a global firm, no single nationality drives the culture, ethos, or leadership of the business.

While this has undoubtedly given the firm local strengths on a global platform, its global reach also means the firm has to work doubly hard to ensure a consistent approach. This means that engaging with lawyers and employees across global frontiers has been a key priority. Baker & McKenzie has relished this challenge, frequently standing out as a leading employer in the industry. Its innovative approach to employee engagement has been the subject of two *Harvard Business Review* studies, and it is the only law firm in the UK to feature in both the 'Sunday Times Top 100 Best Companies to Work For', and 'The Times Best Graduate Employers'.

On the diversity and inclusion front, it was the highest ranked law firm in 'Stonewall's Employer Equity Index', the UK's top 20 lesbian, gay, and bisexual (LGB) friendly employers, and won an award for 'Best Diversity and Inclusion Programme' during the Managing Partner Forum Awards for Management Excellence. Last year, the *Financial Times* recognised the firm as one of the top three most innovative law firms in Europe.

Baker & McKenzie's people agenda

Gillian Coyle, HR director at Baker & McKenzie, says that as a people business the firm has to commit to and value its people more than ever to ensure its success. The firm's people agenda is therefore central to the overall strategy of the firm.

In the volatile, uncertain, complex, and ambiguous (VUCA) world in which people operate, the concept of the 'overwhelmed employee' is a reality, especially in a firm such as Baker & McKenzie that prides itself on being high performing. Therefore, Baker & McKenzie's focus has been to ensure that, while fostering high performance at every level, 'people feel listened to, supported, and valued, but most importantly that they have a key stake in and are driving our people agenda', states Coyle. 'That's why we have put employee engagement and employee partnership as a top priority and are creating an aspirational employee value proposition.'

Employment engagement has always been a priority for the firm. 'We are proud of being a UK top 100 employer for the last five years, but we want to go further and ensure our people define and drive the culture, working practices, and leadership approach that continue to make us an employer of choice', says Coyle. This is why Baker & McKenzie has asked its people to define its 'employee value proposition'.

The employee value proposition will focus on the ideal working world of Baker & McKenzie and create an aspirational charter that sets out the commitment of the firm to its people. This is a joint people and management committee initiative, and a series of focus groups with all of the departments is giving Baker & McKenzie's employees the opportunity to lead on the people agenda and the opportunity to focus on what's important and valuable to them.

While the employee value proposition is being developed, Baker & McKenzie has already put in place a number of recent initiatives to ensure people are central to the firm's agenda, such as:

- Introduction of a learning academy for partners and bespoke development for employees that takes the focus to one-on-one support, rather than generic skills-based training courses;
- A radical review of Baker & McKenzie's evaluation process so there is less focus on ratings and paperwork and more focus on the development of the person;
- Embedding a best-in-class health and wellbeing programme;
- Taking flexible working to the next stage by focusing on agile working to give people more autonomy on where and how they work;
- Supporting diversity and inclusion initiatives, such as blogs and diversity focus groups and their initiatives; and
- Being the first law firm to appoint a partner as a dedicated 'diversity and inclusion partner'.

Learning and development initiatives

Baker & McKenzie has worked hard over a number of years to embed an effective feedback culture – no easy feat in a law firm environment. But at Baker & McKenzie there's a long tradition of encouraging people to identify their strengths, as well as the strengths of others, together with an understanding of what might be getting in the way of those strengths. Recently, Baker & McKenzie has also introduced a number of learning and development initiatives that are less 'classroom' based and more practical.

Senior associate development centre

In 2013, the firm introduced a two-day senior associate development centre. The aim of the initiative, according to Steve Craggs, head of learning and development, is 'for senior associates to be challenged to push themselves out of their comfort zone, get feedback, and develop their skills'. This programme provides real-life situations, using clients and internal teams that are designed to stretch senior associates and provide them with feedback from partner observers. The process takes place away from their day-to-day work, and it's confidential. Partner observers are impartial, allowing senior associates to try new approaches and receive instant feedback. This means that they can learn new skills in real time that add real value to the individual, and therefore to the business.

Partners' business development academy

In January 2015, the firm also introduced a business development academy for partners. The initiative, which is modelled on a distance MBA, runs during a 15-week period, involving 2 hours per week of studying. This makes it different from typical law firm learning in two ways:

1. It is mostly self-paced distance learning; and
2. It is focused on peer learning groups.

This allows partners to organise their study time and, on the other hand, make use of the most valuable learning resource a lawyer has – their colleagues. Partners are clustered into tutorial groups of eight partners who meet regularly to discuss what they are learning, and to coach, challenge, and encourage each other. The dynamic is similar to the role tutorial groups play in a business or law school setting. Experienced business development (BD) coaches have facilitated these tutorials by guiding partners to share their stories about the things that have worked for them and those that have not.

The academy consists of five modules, each lasting three weeks. These five modules were chosen based on partners' own views of their biggest needs: generating leads, market profile raising, fee negotiation through creative pricing structures, creating deeper client relationships, and responding to market trends.

Steve Craggs says that one of the concepts behind the academy was to give partners more time for reflection. 'Too often in law firms there is a focus on planning and doing things, but not enough reflection afterwards as to whether the process worked. The academy gives partners that time to reflect and hopefully engages them to build reflection time into processes in the future.'

Coaching

Alongside these major initiatives, Baker & McKenzie has also taken a step forward in its use of coaching techniques by creating a panel of 20 in-house coaches who are updated on all important issues within Baker & McKenzie, and who work closely with lawyers. By having a small panel of coaches, they are more closely aligned in their way of operating, and this allows for a better work structure.

Agile working

One of Baker & McKenzie's key strategic aims is to ensure that it upholds and maximises a culture that is collaborative, fulfilling, diverse, and inclusive. With this in mind, Baker & McKenzie engaged in a flexible working scheme that could benefit and satisfy employees' needs. Coinciding with the new shared parental leave (SPL) legislation which came into effect December 2014, the firm decided to support working parents who take SPL by offering some enhanced pay. Under this new approach:

- Mothers/primary adopters are to be paid up to 26 weeks full pay during leave – this can be paid in the first 26 weeks of maternity/adoption leave or they can choose to receive up to 12 weeks' pay during SPL and have fewer paid for maternity/adoption;
- Partners who qualify for SPL are able to take up to 12 weeks of shared parental leave on full pay, inclusive of two weeks paternity pay; and
- Partners who do not qualify for SPL may be entitled to two weeks paternity pay.

In order to offer maximum flexibility to parents to help manage their childcare responsibilities, the 12 weeks of SPL with pay can be taken at any time within a 52 week period following the birth/adoption of a child and does not have to be taken as a continuous block of leave. This approach differentiates Baker & McKenzie from many of its competitors. Baker & McKenzie is moving towards an agile working model, where in addition to the structured flexible working scheme already in place, our people have more individual autonomy on their working lives and their roles are more agile so they can achieve better work-life balance.

Diversity and inclusion

Diversity and inclusion has always been one of Baker & McKenzie's guiding principles. The firm strongly believes that an inclusive and diverse environment is an asset that supports its peoples' personal and professional growth and development. As evidence of this, the firm appointed Sarah Gregory, a senior employment partner at Baker & McKenzie as its first partner for diversity and inclusion in July 2014. The firm believes having a partner solely dedicated to this role is unique in the market.

Baker & McKenzie's diversity focus groups are key to driving the office inclusion and diversity strategy. Recently, the firm added a new focus group – BakerWellbeing – to its growing list. The firm has also focused heavily on social mobility and engages all of its people to participate in different activities.

Appointing a diversity and inclusion partner

Retaining and developing a diverse talent pool is a key business issue for Baker & McKenzie, and it is one of its key strategic aims in the office and in the firm more generally. In order to sustain its position and make further progress, the diversity and inclusion area required leadership and focus at dedicated partner level. Therefore, Sarah Gregory, a partner specialising in employment at Baker & McKenzie for over 15 years, changed her focus and undertook a newly created role as diversity and inclusion partner for the London office. Sarah's appointment seemed a very natural choice, as she had chaired the London office diversity committee for a number of years before moving into this role. The role of diversity and inclusion partner was a new one for Baker & McKenzie, and also within the UK legal market as a whole. The creation of this dedicated, partner-level role reflects the deep commitment that Baker & McKenzie has, and has always had, to inclusion and diversity. The role involves Sarah Gregory in every aspect of the business, from recruitment, retention, and promotion of staff, to work with clients, and to dealings with suppliers.

Diversity focus groups

Baker & McKenzie initially launched five diversity employee networks a number of years ago: BakerBalance, BakerEthnicity, BakerLGBT (lesbian, gay, bisexual, transgender), BakerOpportunity, and BakerWomen. Recently, it added BakerWellbeing to its roster of staff focus groups. Not only do the groups provide an excellent network for staff at all levels across the office, but they are also designed as 'vehicles for change', with ideas and opinions raised by the groups directly impacting overall strategy. Outcomes so far have included:

- A new and more comprehensive emergency back-up scheme covering children, elder care, and individual care as a result of recommendations from BakerBalance;
- A more flexible shared parental leave policy application as a result of recommendations from BakerBalance;
- Introducing a global LGBT policy as a result of recommendations by BakerLGBT;
- Creation of an LGBT 'listening ear scheme' as a result of recommendations by BakerLGBT;
- Signing up to the Social Mobility Business Compact, and becoming contextual recruitment pioneers as a result of recommendations by BakerOpportunity;
- Developing initiatives to get men involved in gender discussions following recommendations from BakerWomen; and
- A comprehensive review of the firm's graduate recruitment process, resulting in a significant increase in the number of BME (black and minority ethnic) trainee recruits following recommendations from BakerEthnicity.

Activities and communications for each of the diversity focus groups play a big role in

Baker & McKenzie, involving many members of staff, lawyers, and partners. A proactive diversity communications campaign has been rolled out and, as a result, powerful personal accounts on social mobility, LGBT, ethnicity, and gender were shared by staff and partners, including Paul Rawlinson, London managing partner at Baker & McKenzie, and Tom Cassels, global head of dispute resolution.

Global LGBT policy

Baker & McKenzie launched a global LGBT policy to be applied by all Baker & McKenzie offices worldwide (even those in jurisdictions typically known as being challenging for LGBT people). The initiative implies zero tolerance to any form of homophobic harassment or bullying and strongly encourages equalisation of benefits for same-sex couples. In order for it to have a greater impact within the firm, the global LGBT policy was communicated by Eduardo Leite, Baker & McKenzie's global chairman. Each office within Baker & McKenzie now has an LGBT liaison partner, responsible for ensuring the global policy is adhered to.

Baker & McKenzie is ahead of the curve when it comes to LGBT business issues. The firm believes straight allies have a crucial role to play in creating LGBT-friendly environments. In its London office, Baker & McKenzie has more than 300 people in its LGBT allies network; almost one third of the office population.

Social mobility and diversity

One of the issues that Baker & McKenzie has been particularly keen to promote is social mobility – meaning not only attracting and recruiting people from diverse backgrounds, but also creating an internal environment in which they can thrive. The social mobility focus group reviews initiatives, identifies gaps in the programme, and monitors progress to suggest new and more innovative approaches. The group has outlined a comprehensive strategy with measurable aims and objectives to span outreach, access and recruitment, career development, monitoring, and profile/communications.

The firm has longstanding relationships with a number of organisations aiming to raise the aspirations of young people from less privileged backgrounds, including the Social Mobility Foundation, Enabling Enterprise, Pure Potential, Lawyers in Schools, and Career Ready. The firm has also forged strong relationships with sixth form colleges in greater and outer London suburbs, very specifically aiming to reach students at schools and colleges in economically deprived areas who do not already benefit from support and interventions from City employers.

However, the firm felt it could also go further. In January 2014, Baker & McKenzie introduced its inaugural 'social mobility week', aimed at raising awareness around social mobility issues both within the firm and in the external market. Adopting a 'Contextual Recruitment System' which monitors the academic performance of candidates in an efficient way that takes into consideration their background. The initiatives are about more than being 'nice' (a term in Baker & McKenzie's development framework), they are about building a strong baseline fit for the 21st century.

Health and wellbeing

Recently, Baker & McKenzie launched the BakerWellbeing focus group, an initiative aiming to support the health and wellbeing of all staff and partners. As part of the firm's commitment to creating a culture that supports and encourages healthy lifestyles, BakerWellbeing brings together the range of health and wellbeing benefits that Baker & McKenzie offers to employees, and it provides information on how they can get support both internally and externally.

The initiative is composed of four pillars fundamental to fulfilling and maintaining a healthy lifestyle, which are: mental resilience, diet, exercise, and health. For each of these, Baker & McKenzie brings in speakers to talk about issues or advice on different health and wellbeing topics; arranges in-house activities for employees to join; sets up discussion panels; and provides an employee assistance programme (EAP), which is a confidential advice service that provides practical and emotional support. The EAP offers a free telephone service that is available 24 hours a day, seven days a week, and gives access to specialist advice and information, confidential telephone counselling when the employee is in need of talking to someone, and up to six face-to-face counselling sessions.

Conclusion

All of the initiatives have contributed to achieving an environment that allows the people at Baker & McKenzie to grow professional and personally, and to feel truly engaged with the firm. As a result of the initiatives undertaken by the firm, the engagement score in Baker & McKenzie is 5 per cent above the global professional services norm, and 2 per cent more than global high-performing norms. Baker & McKenzie want to take their people agenda to a different level. Rather than merely implementing the next big HR initiative, the firm is asking its people to define the agenda, and to tell the firm what they want, expect, and need to stay truly engaged.

Case study 2: Marque Lawyers – The development of law firm innovation

By Michael Bradley, managing partner at Marque Lawyers

MARQUE LAWYERS will turn seven this year, and while we've grown and matured considerably as a business over that time, perhaps our staff have not really changed. (It occurred to me recently, when the head of our corporate/M&A practice, Kristy Dixon, brought Savvy in for an 'office dog day', that the dog is actually more mature than most of our employees.) The truth is that having fun has been one of our values since we started, and we remain violently committed to it.

The office currently has the appearance of a post-modern art exhibition as it's filled with the results of our recent clerkship recruitment campaign. (Once the law students had worked out what we meant when we demanded applications 'by diorama', they responded with some alarming creativity.) There is meanwhile much excitement as we approach our next regular workstation rotation in which we draw lots to determine who our immediate neighbours will be for the next six months. And that also means bubble soccer (YouTube it).

I could be accused of painting an unrealistic picture of life at our law firm by selectively picking out just a few fun bits, but in truth I only had to think a couple of weeks in either direction to come up with that list. For us, having fun is no less serious a part of our business plan than collecting the debts (and I genuinely don't care whether or not you believe that). Quite simply, we think that those who enjoy their work, work better, and are more motivated in the long term – which is why, seven years ago, we set out to do law differently.

Marque, seven years on

Reflecting on where Marque sits in the night sky now, what I find most remarkable is how little we've changed. The firm is bigger, more materially successful, and is doing ever more interesting work for more interesting clients. We have also become increasingly sophisticated in our thinking and approach to the bigger challenges like workplace flexibility, the needs of working parents, the aspirations of Gen Y, and the perennial question of how to maintain a culture of openness and the optimistic embrace of change.

So, there is plenty happening and we haven't lost any of our enthusiasm for what's next. What I mean when I say 'we haven't changed' is that we have the same values and purpose we had at the outset, and we have never felt the slightest pressure or temptation to deviate from them. That's been revelatory. Running a business is so much more enjoyable when you know why you're doing it.

Marque's purpose, in case it needs restating, is to innovate and revolutionise the way law is practised. We've spent the past seven years constantly refining our own business model as we have deepened our understanding of what makes people want to give more to a relationship – staff and clients alike. It's been fascinating.

The pressure of competition (or not)

Equally fascinating is the marketplace in

which we've been busily going about our reinvention. I'm often asked about who we see as our competition. Has anyone been copying us? Do I think any other firm will do what we're doing? The short answer is no.

Competition is not actually something we spend any time contemplating or discussing. Not because we're so arrogant as to think that we're immune from the laws of the market; we understand the principles of marketing. It's just that law firms, like many businesses, tend to think about competitors merely as something against which to benchmark their firm – and then try to make sure they're not falling behind the trends. That's a sure way to guarantee that you'll never innovate. The only good reason to keep an eye on your competitors is to help identify how you might differentiate your own offering. (Benchmarking, in my opinion, is a stupid pursuit.)

As to whether we're being copied or will be, our attitude is who really cares? Our most visible differentiators are the way we charge for our services and our refusal to take it all too seriously, and they're not too difficult to emulate if you want to. But the true difference cannot be replicated. We are ruthlessly authentic – honest about ourselves, sincere about everything we say, outspoken on the things we care about – and you can't copy that. You can only ever authentically be yourself. That means that Marque can't be replicated, although it doesn't mean that it can't be bettered.

So, if everyone in the legal services market isn't lying awake at night wondering how they can be more like Marque, then what is happening out there?

External forces impacting the legal market

I see three perspectives from which the state of the market can be examined: external forces; innovation in the legal market; and what the legacy firms are doing about all this.

Outside of the firms, two major pressure points are gradually building. First, there is the glacial rate at which clients, particularly corporate counsel, are coming to realise just how much market power they have. The talk tends to focus on cost-cutting pressure, but that's always been a fact of corporate life and hasn't ever really impacted much on legal spend (because clients have been educated to accept that legal spend is an unknowable and unmanageable risk).

The real issue is the ability of clients to dictate to their lawyers what they will pay. I've never quite understood why this isn't more obvious to clients. It's pretty simple: with rare exceptions, the legal market is over-supplied and clients have complete mobility. The fact is, there are plenty of good lawyers out there with the right expertise, and they're all desperate for market share. Which means that clients have enormous buying power.

As clients gain a greater appreciation of the balance of power between them and their lawyers, they will put increasing pressure on firms. At present, this tends to be focused on the meaningless quest to keep hourly rates down – meaningless because that only provides more incentives for inefficiency, over-servicing, and plain fraud. Clients do not save money by pushing rates down. (There, I said it.)

The more savvy clients are taking a longer perspective on the more important questions of relationship and value. Hourly rates are a measure of cost, which ought to be irrelevant to clients. They should care less about how much it costs us to do their work, or what profit margin we get, and focus instead on the long-term value they derive for the total amount they spend. As clients place more emphasis on value, and ask ever more difficult questions about how their lawyers plan to deliver it, it will become increasingly apparent that the traditional law firm business model is ill-designed for that purpose. As it is driven solely by multiplying hours by a (made-up) figure, it focuses everyone's attention on recovering a set return for each hour. That has nothing whatever to do with the value of what each person is doing, either in the abstract or in the context of the client's needs. In the end, law firms who cling to the time costing model will be unable to effectively respond to the demands of the marketplace. They're offering the wrong service.

The second pressure point is generational. To me it's very clear that each succeeding generation is demonstrating decreasing willingness to suffer now for the promise of future gain. I readily accept that my own generation (X) largely thinks that that's just because Gen Y is 'spoiled' and doesn't understand the need for hard work. I just don't agree. There's a much deeper philosophical debate to be had here. My summary of it is that the corporate paradigm which has ruled for most of the past century is now past its use-by date. The mindless pursuit of profit as an end in itself was always devoid of meaning. We all seek meaning from our lives, including from the work we do, and the younger generations are simply being noisier and more demanding about that quest. They want what they're entitled to – a sense of purpose in what they do.

Translating that to the world of law firms, consider the prospect law graduates face. A law degree has become the entry requirement into a factory job, albeit one with harbour views and gym membership. But it is a factory. Young lawyers immediately learn about the one thing which will define each day and determine their success or failure: their timesheet. Six minute units are the measure of recognition and reward. They may get great work, impressive clients, good pay, perks, and social status. They have the prospect of promotion if they stick it out. But all of that is secondary to the absolute requirement that their timesheet is continually fed.

I'm not saying that people can't derive meaning from a bargain that entails hard work, even exploitation, in return for potential future benefits. They can. Look at the acting profession. My point is that this can only really work if what is held up as of value is something that is actually of meaning to you. Nobody can derive meaning from charging hours, and yet that is how law firms measure value.

This isn't a problem with which law firms currently need to concern themselves, because there is a seemingly endless queue of hopeful new lawyers willing to accept any bargain just so they can get a start. But still, I can't see a happy long-term future for a business in which there is no alignment between the institutionalised measures of value and the human desires and needs of its workforce. (I know, salt mines can operate for many decades on exactly that basis. That's why I included the word 'happy'.)

Innovation in the law, or what passes for it

Turning to innovation in the legal market, legal process outsourcing (LPO) made a big splash initially. Now it is quietly growing and finding its place. Some big law firms, having decided that this is an enemy they can't beat, have been seeking to co-opt LPOs into the role of sub-contractors. If it isn't happening already, global firms will start to self-insure by buying or establishing their own captive LPOs.

There are many types of legal work that can be done by LPOs or similar low-cost providers. This is the work that has always made the big law firm business model super-profitable. The model relies on leverage – large numbers of junior lawyers and paralegals being charged by the hour at many multiples of their salaries, for what is essentially process work. The biggest earners are litigation discovery and due diligence for corporate transactions. They can be done just as effectively and many times more cheaply if outsourced. The price can also be fixed; there's no good reason for it to be charged on a time basis.

Another innovation is contract placement; there are many new 'firms' who place lawyers inside clients on contract for specific purposes. This is proving popular with clients, and we'll see more of it. A few big firms have also noticed, and are trying to get into the contractor game themselves. My personal view is that cannibalising your own business (i.e. competing against yourself) is a dangerous strategy.

As for the so-called 'New Law' firms, good on them. Most, so far, aren't that much different from traditional firms in reality, but I think there is a positive trend towards more authentically different offerings coming to the market.

Meanwhile, as Rome burns

Finally, what are the legacy firms doing? Mostly, exactly what you'd expect legacy businesses to be doing. Here's what I think we're seeing and will see more of:

- A race to the 'top' – With too many big firms competing for a decreasing pool of work, they know that not all will survive. Some will respond by trying to grow to a dominant position, to ensure they are one of the survivors. Their role model for this is the victory of the Big Four accounting firms, which was achieved by constant merging and global expansion. The arrival of so many global mega firms in Australia is one indicator that numerous law firms are trying to achieve the same outcome.
- Merger mania – There's going to be a lot more of this, including some monster mergers between global behemoths.
- Poaching bonanza – The big firms have been poaching each other's big-earning partners in ever increasing numbers, and this is going to ramp up even more. The global firms are accelerating this with their deeper balance sheets, creating havoc in smaller markets like Australia.
- Fewer jobs for junior lawyers – This has been a dramatic shift in Australia; big firms have cut their graduate intake, as they narrow out their base and seek to hold on to the more profitable middle-level lawyers. It's consistent both with their push to reduce overheads and their drive towards securing more higher-level and higher-margin legal work (for which you need more senior lawyers).
- Ever more refinement of the existing business model – It ain't broke, so nobody really wants to move away from time costing. Insteac, law firms are working constantly harder on squeezing every possible penny out of it.

It's a truly fascinating and exciting time to be a lawyer. Our industry is dominated by participants dedicated to refining a business model which has made them a lot of money for many years. What they're ignoring is that it became obsolete some time ago. Once you appreciate that, what looked like an overcrowded market opens up into a big field of opportunity. I'm confident that we're not the only lawyers who are seeing it.

In the meantime, bubble soccer beckons.

About the author

Michael Bradley is the managing partner of Marque Lawyers, a boutique commercial law firm in Sydney which he and some fellow refugees from Big Law founded in 2008 with the stated intention of completely revolutionising the way law is practised. Anyone who has had anything to do with Marque will attest that it really does do law differently. Apart from continuing to explore how much fun a lawyer can have while pretending to work, Michael writes regularly on public interest issues, the legal industry, and whatever else he gets excited about. He also wrote a book called *Kill all the Lawyers,* which pretty much sums it all up.

Case study 3: AdventBalance – Innovation and value at the heart of everything we do

Interview with John Knox, managing director, Asia at AdventBalance

Things have obviously changed since Advent Lawyers were featured in ARK Group's first innovation report back in 2011. How do you think the merger and formation of AdventBalance has affected your value proposition and how you work?
The merger we thought would provide clients with a better, more well-rounded, offering. Although the two businesses pre-merger were doing similar things, the client bases were different. So the rationale was really to create more scale and a wider lawyer group, skill set, and a broader geographic footprint. We now also have a more diverse client base. It has enhanced our value to clients and, from a HR perspective, it has enhanced our proposition to staff as they now get to work with a wider group of people across different offices and from different backgrounds. The feedback from our people has been extremely positive.

It is clear that you focus on innovation and not on following the status quo for legal services delivery. But what does it mean to have 'innovation and value at the heart of everything' you do (as per your website)? What exactly is 'innovation' to you?
'Innovation' is one of those words that is very overused. Our aim is is to do things differently for clients. It is about efficiency and cost-effectiveness, and our culture is at the heart of everything we do. We really try to think about what will benefit clients when we make decisions within the business. We ask, 'what will clients get out of this?', or 'is it efficient'? The second part of that to us – and it may not sound like innovation – is thinking about what it means for our own people and culture. Our flexibility and variety, how we work, connectedness and remote working – all of these are important and breed a level of entrepreneurialism and innovation in how we behave as a team.

So you promote innovation and thinking outside the box amongst your people?
Yes, absolutely. When you think about it, the benefit we had, unlike traditional law firms working with a set business model and trying to innovate around it, is that we started with a blank piece of paper and to this day we are still designing what we do and how we do it. It is a lot easier for us to innovate as we are building from the ground up. Our structure also helps with innovation. We have a corporatised structure with a group of shareholders and a board, and we don't need to bounce decisions off 400 partners across a range of offices. We involve people in decisions and everyone's input counts, but it does mean we can action good ideas very quickly.

In ARK Group's 2011 report, the fixed fee was outlined as the central focus of an innovative legal services offering in the Advent Lawyers case study. Does this remain the same for AdventBalance? Are fixed fees still a big focus for you?
Yes, nearly everything we do is fixed fee. But our approach is less about fixed fees and more about budget certainty. What clients

really want, in our opinion, is to get a quote for a piece of work and for it to come in at that price so they then don't have to go to their CFO, CEO, or managing director and explain why something was way over budget. We give budget certainty to clients. We bill clients on a month-by-month basis and they will always know what that bill is going to be before they see it as they have engaged us on that basis. So yes it is fixed fee, but what is more important is budget certainty and no surprises.

The two other concepts that are really important for us are:

- Transparency (which is not dissimilar from budget certainty in a way). We are not afraid to be upfront and honest with clients about what we are delivering and what we are not delivering on what we are offering, and what it will look like. From the outset there is always an alignment of expectations.
- Flexibility is the other thing. Again, maybe that is easier under our corporate structure than it would be under a global partnership, but I think clients would generally say that we are very flexible.

So, really, it is not just about fixed fees. It is about budget certainty, transparency, and flexibility.

It may seem obvious, but in your own words can you give some specific examples of how you differ from the traditional law firm?

There are a number of things. The first is that our lawyers sit with our clients. So our model is different. We are working closely with our clients and that really helps with the transparency aspect. They're real-time and in the offices (so the clients know what they are getting), and that's a big difference.

The second is our cost structure, and our minimal overheads. If you come and look at our offices and premises and compare them to what you get with a traditional law firm, they are very different. We don't pay our people any less, but where we have trimmed costs in the model is in the overheads and a lot of that has to do with premises.

The third area, which I have already talked about, is our corporate structure with shareholders and a board as opposed to a partnership model. We are not the only ones with this kind of model, but incorporated legal structures are still few and far between.

The other area where we are truly different is work-life balance and encouraging women at different stages in their careers to get back into the law. We genuinely deliver on that, and it's not just lip service for us. There are real statistics to demonstrate that. For example, 63 per cent of our total workforce work flexibly, and 70 per cent are female. There are a range of other factors, but these are the key concepts that differentiate us.

Considering what you mentioned about your culture and work-life balance as part of your offering, do you think it affects your clients that you have certain types of lawyers at AdventBalance? Does employee satisfaction affect them?

Absolutely. The feedback we get on our people and the fact they have lives outside of law is positive. As part of our interview process, we like to ask people what they do outside of work. We have very rounded individuals. Does that come through and benefit the client? Yes, I think it does.

Are you successful because you are innovative? Or do you see it as just one aspect?

It is not just innovation. Innovation is a large part of it – we have designed a successful new business model – but why we are successful on an ongoing basis is because we are efficient and cost effective in what we do. We maintain the focus on quality, we employ highly skilled people, and we pay them appropriately. I think the main reason clients come back to us is because we are efficient and we pass cost savings on to them. The end result is that clients get the same product as they would from a traditional law firm, but do it in a far more cost effective way. We are successful because we have innovated in this sense. We structured our business and the way we practise based on two very simple questions: what our lawyers want; and what our clients want.

In terms of innovation and clients, do clients actually ask you much about innovation? Do they refer to it at all?

Clients don't refer to innovation itself that often, but yes they see us as different, and a bit unique. It's actually the other way around. Our conversations with clients involve us asking them how they want us to practise, rather than them raising innovation with us. That is the secret to our success – we have structured a business based on what lawyers and clients want, and we marry those two together.

You were shortlisted in the Best Leadership of Innovation category as part of the 2015 Managing Partners Forum Awards for Management Excellence. Do you think innovation in a firm needs to come from the top?

These things do come from the top in part. If the managing director and CEO are behaving in one way and saying the firm operates in another, then there is obviously a disconnect. But another factor is that we try to recruit people who are energetic and want to be part of something that is entrepreneurial and innovative. I think a lot of it comes from the team, and we do not work on a strict top-down approach.

How innovative is the legal market in the Asia-Pacific? How much do you think it compares to the US or the UK, and do you focus on what is happening in other markets?

I think you need to break down the Asia-Pacific. Australia is definitely ahead of Asia in terms of the regulation of law and what that enables the market to do. I think parts of Asia are taking steps in the right direction. You can now have a corporatised structure in Singapore, but you can't in Hong Kong (although there is a paper in front of their law society at the moment addressing those issues). It is not a criticism of Asia, but I think Australia is more at the forefront of innovation. It comes down to regulatory reform and culture.

The UK is even further ahead than Australia. That comes down to regulation more than anything – allowing corporatised entities to practise law, and non-legal owners and capital has made a huge difference. All innovation stems from structure, and the old structures adopted by traditional firms do not easily lend themselves to giving clients what they want these days – or giving lawyers what they want.

Do we keep abreast of the changes? Absolutely, we are always reading up on what is happening in overseas markets and we find that clients often want to talk about that sort of stuff. We are prepared to discuss it at client meetings and to help them to understand what is happening in the market.

What lies ahead for AdventBalance?

We have a clear vision to expand and grow the business further. In saying that, we do not believe in growth for growth's sake and we want to maintain our unique culture and the same focus on quality that differentiates us. We will continue listening to clients and the service offerings they want. We will continue to design the business around what clients want us to offer them. We will stay flexible and nimble with our variable cost base, and we can design our offering based on that.

Case study 4: gunnercooke – Innovation in a very different law firm

By Darryl Cooke, founder of gunnercooke

'I DON'T feel like I can hear a clock ticking in the background when I need to call and ask a question', said one of our clients, a head of legal at a listed UK retail group. I'd asked him about what felt different about being a client of gunnercooke, the corporate and commercial law firm my business partner, Sarah Goulbourne, and I founded nearly four and a half years ago. Happily, he's not alone in this sentiment; this week we welcomed our 2,000th client at gunnercooke, along with our 77th partner.

When we set out to build gunnercooke, we had a very simple belief that legal services could be delivered in a better way that would benefit our clients and also the lawyers that we would recruit. I had worked for many years as partner and head of private equity at some of the world's largest firms, and had long since felt the pressure of balancing increasing hourly billing targets with people management, international bureaucracy, oh and delivering client service as well. My partner Sarah sat on the other side of the fence, as general counsel in a number of FTSE 250 companies, including Stanley Leisure plc and Trinity Publishing plc. Sarah had been on the receiving end of 'surprise' bills, client 'relationship' managers that turn up once a year to ask for more work, and partners who sold an experienced trusted advisor service, which was delivered by 1–2 year qualified lawyers. She'd been the quality controller on one too many legal documents, checking the work of external lawyers for the accuracy and commerciality that only comes with having been round the block a few times.

I'd met Sarah a number of times over the years, and we'd often spoken about our frustrations of an industry bound by tradition, hierarchy, and halted progression due to an overreliance on democratic decision making. By 2010, Sarah had gained her MBA, and having recently lost my father, who I'd spoken with about my ambitions at length, I felt like it was time to put words into action, and do something that would change the way that legal services worked for my clients.

We approached our target audience – CEOs, FDs, HOLs, and financiers of businesses – and asked each of them the same question: 'If you set out to create the perfect law firm, what would it look like?' Their responses gave us the basis of the gunnercooke model. Much as our personal experience had told us, clients wanted senior lawyers who could advise with expertise, authority, and commercial nous. Perhaps more importantly, they also wanted a greater degree of transparency over what these services would cost.

The gunnercooke model

To this end, we set up gunnercooke to be a senior lawyer only firm. We call it our 10,000 hour rule, which is the minimum amount of time that leading business writer Malcolm Gladwell states it takes to become an expert in any field. Every lawyer at gunnercooke has a minimum of 10,000 hours practising experience from leading national and international firms or senior in-house legal positions. Not only this, another differentiator between our firm and our competitors is that over 90 per cent of gunnercooke lawyers have spent time in business, or in-house. This factor is very important to us, because it means that our lawyers have a greater appreciation for the impact of their legal advice on the wider business. Technical genius only serves as one element of being a great lawyer; commerciality, ability to form relationships, to act as a true trusted advisor, these are all attributes that we felt should embody any partner of gunnercooke.

The fixed-fee model seemed to sit naturally alongside this recruitment strategy. The idea of time recording has always bothered me; it seems to encourage inefficiency. Why complete work in two hours when you can charge more for doing it in three? One client in our initial research exercise noted:

> *'When a decorator is painting your house, you can see where he starts, and make an assessment on how fast he is, how accurate. If, at the end of a week, he says that he needs a week longer than expected and therefore there is a greater charge – I understand it, and I can rationalise whether it's fair or not. With a lawyer it's different. I can't tell how much time they've taken; I don't know whether they're a slow worker, whether they spend a lot of time out of the office, or whether their work is as accurate as it can be. When they feed back that a contract has taken 30 hours longer than expected and my fee has doubled, I have no idea whether that's fair.'*

When we set up gunnercooke, we abolished the use of time sheets. As every lawyer that joins is a senior practitioner, they have a much greater sense of the value that they can add to a client's requirement, and the work involved. We coach our lawyers on 'value-based' pricing, and stress the importance of establishing the scope of work from the outset, because once the fee is agreed, it cannot change.

Sometimes, especially in tenders for public sector work, we are pushed to give an hourly rate, simply so the authority can assess gunnercooke in line with other providers, but I see this changing in time. Four years ago, fixed legal fees were a very new concept for corporate and commercial lawyers. Some may have professed to be offering this while inserting heavy caveats, assumptions, ifs, and buts. The term 'fixed' is one that we've had to educate on, as it can bring connotations of 'cheap'. We haven't tried to gain a foothold in the market by offering cheap legal services, we just seek to offer them in a way that gives greater certainty and value to the client.

Expansion and growth

In our first year, we gained a number of corporate plc clients in retail, waste management, and construction: companies that bought into the idea of seniority and certainty, and saw that we could deliver. We recruited five corporate partners. Having initially been apprehensive about how the market would respond to our fresh ideas, already our progress is exciting. Everyone we spoke to agreed that the model resonated, and we began to implement a strategy for growth, working closely with recruitment partners to seek out lawyers who had reached a certain level in firms, who had become frustrated with the more traditional model and were ready to try something a little more innovative. Unsurprisingly, they weren't difficult to find.

Lawyers at gunnercooke are remunerated on a fee share model, meaning they are paid for the work that they deliver, and contribute a percentage of their fees to investment in the central business operation. This helps to ensure that the client pays for the advice of the lawyer, not for the running of our business; our fees are agreed at levels that constitute better value for the client. Our lawyers each have their own business plan and it remains fundamentally important to us that we create an environment that encourages flexibility, innovation, and collaboration.

Our systems have been developed securely through the cloud, and our offices in London and Manchester are set up as business hubs, with hot-desks, meeting rooms, and space for lawyers to get together and share ideas. We've invested each year in strengthening a back office team to support our lawyers in finance, insurance, marketing, branding, technology, and business planning. They are all trained to see our lawyers as their clients; we want gunnercooke to be a service-led organisation at its very core, so our team is trained first and foremost in ways to provide brilliant service.

Culture

I paint a picture of the perfect environment and I would, wouldn't I? Yet the point I wish to emphasise is the importance of culture. In the traditional firm, bureaucratic though it is, there is a strong sense of tradition that I admire, and we wanted gunnercooke to be instilled with the better aspects of those values, while operating in a totally different environment.

gunnercooke is an amalgamation of talent from some of the greatest law firms in the world and, at this point in time, around 50 per cent of our partners have been with the firm for less than 18 months. When you consider it in those terms, it's vital that we place such a huge focus on instilling our brand and culture throughout the firm. We have a very active social programme to help people get to know each other, and our team meetings take the form of group discussions – on pricing, client service, or operating in the model – to encourage people to air challenges and solutions with each other.

We've been able to form strategies around our different practice areas, focusing on both celebrating our points of difference, and exploring the way that our teams deliver service together. There is no hierarchy in our model. No-one is cracking a whip; there's no competing to lead on the biggest client accounts. We don't have heads of department, and so team strategies are underpinned by our values – values that every lawyer in our firm must share. I blog every week to our partners to tell them about our progress, to continuously instil our vision. That's how we believe we'll maintain cohesion between our lawyers: by continuing to emphasise the importance of our culture.

Every year since its inception, our business has doubled in size, and last year our revenue grew by 143 per cent. It's much easier now for us to talk to senior lawyers in some of the best firms, as many lawyers are struggling to adapt to the new economy in a traditional model. The race to reach partnership doesn't hold the attraction it once did, and increasingly we see the CVs of lawyers in their early thirties – ambitious, entrepreneurial, and hungry to try something different.

We won't accept everyone. Our vision to be the 'best' is centred on service and quality, not numbers. Our vision is extremely ambitious, but we have to focus on building the best environment for our lawyers and the best service for our clients. We're not there yet. I often say to our partners that, in terms of development, we're a three out of ten, maybe even a two. In a people business, our service is only as good as our people. So we have to keep pushing ourselves; we won't get complacent. Every experience that the market has of gunnercooke contributes to the way that people will label our brand. I'm very aware of that, and I'm very driven by it. Our journey has only just begun.

About the author

Darryl Cooke is the founder of gunnercooke. He is renowned as a private equity lawyer, having worked in the industry for over 25 years. In that time, he's helped clients to invest, buy, sell, and raise money for businesses across the UK and all over the world, even writing the world's leading book on the subject. He is passionate about ensuring that legal processes evolve to meet the changing requirements of funders and of the fast-growing businesses that they invest in.

Case study 5: Riverview Law – The coming storm

By Karl Chapman, chief executive, Riverview Law

Real and imaginary barriers

In the last few years I've led a business in the legal market for the first time; Riverview Law was launched on 20 February 2012. Unsurprisingly, perhaps, I've often felt like an outsider, an intruder. Separated by the language, the behaviours, the myths. The aura surrounding the rule of law, law firms, and lawyers. Those real and imaginary barriers carefully constructed over generations.

At first I rationalised my feelings as those of the newcomer – with all the advantages and disadvantages that this brings. All I had to do, I thought, was to listen and learn. I'd soon work out what was happening. After all, I'd had similar feelings when we entered the recruitment market in 1989 and the HR advisory outsourcing market in 2000.

As with law, these were markets in which we had no previous experience before we set up our businesses. We just saw big markets, at change points, with unsatisfied customer demand and a fragmented and undercapitalised supply chain. We saw opportunity that we could hopefully realise by keeping things simple, and by focusing on delivering a great service to customers at a fair price. We were prepared to take calculated risks and back our judgments with capital, energy, and experimentation.

From Law 1.0 to Law 3.0

But, as the CodeX April 2015 FutureLaw Conference at Stanford Law School proved, the legal world is different – fundamentally so. The excellent speakers and delegates at that conference helped draw together some thoughts that have consciously and unconsciously driven Riverview Law forward.

The opening address at CodeX was delivered by Professor Oliver Goodenough. His subject was 'The State of the Art of Legal Technology Circa 2015'. He gave an overview of legal technology, focusing on the various systemic changes confronting the law and legal practice. However, it was how he described the different technological approaches that the various stakeholders in the legal system have been adopting to respond to these changes that made things click.

To make his point, he kept it simple. He used the now clichéd, but as he rightly said still useful terms of 1.0, 2.0, and 3.0. His summary was (and apologies to Oliver if I've misquoted him):

- In Law 1.0 technology empowers the current human players within the current system;
- In Law 2.0 technology becomes disruptive because it replaces an increasing number of the human players, but again within the current system and operating model; but
- In Law 3.0 we see a radical re-design and, to a greater or lesser extent, the replacement of the current system with a new system driven by the power of computational technology and new entrants.

1989

Of course, this transition can be applied to any number of other markets: the impact of online shopping on retailing, automation in car manufacturing, Uber and airbnb. But there are some catches here for legal, and not just the obvious ones that most incumbents are largely stuck in 1.0, and that many new entrants (particularly the technology companies) are looking to substitute them and deliver Law 3.0, rather than help incumbents become Law 2.0.

Many (particularly lawyers) would argue that the legal market is facing something like a perfect storm in the UK following the Legal Services Act 2007, the economic meltdown in 2008, the increasing shift in buying power to the customer, and increased competition. But I have always thought that this is a narrow and flawed analysis. Firstly, it confuses regulatory and economic events as the key drivers. In practice the really big themes are that customers have, finally, had enough. And technology is changing the rules of engagement. Put simply, consumers and businesses have paid too much for legal services and there is a crisis in access to justice.

Secondly, and most critically, it identifies the wrong date. It wasn't 2007/2008 that triggered the perfect storm. The winds of change bringing in the coming big storm – because today is just a minor shower compared with what happens next – began to blow in 1989 when Tim Berners-Lee created the first web browser.

The big problem for the legal industry is that it is now having to fight on two fronts, not that many players recognise this. Yes, it is experiencing its own vertical market re-structuring, which is driving Law 1.0 to Law 2.0 (about time). And a lot of the legal sector in the UK and in the US is not well positioned to manage this single challenge given the partnership model, weak balance sheets, and the culture of law firms. However, and some might say unluckily, at the same time the legal market has to contend with a technology revolution that is profound and that will impact all sectors of the economy. A revolution that has been over 25 years in the making, from when Tim Berners-Lee invented the internet in 1989, to the first commercial web browser in 1993 (Mosaic), through the dotcom boom and bust between 1995 and 2000, and the creation of Google in 2008... It is a revolution that spans big data, through the cloud, to artificial intelligence. To keep things simple, and focusing on its consequences – its output – I'll describe this revolution as 'the rise of the knowledge worker'.

The rise of the knowledge worker

The technological revolution we're living through will affect all of us and impact all sectors of the economy and society. Its language includes many current buzz words: big data, the internet of things, expert systems, deep automation, artificial intelligence, blockchains, computational law, the cloud. However, and cutting through the terminology to focus on its practical consequences, one of the key themes in this period will be the rise of the knowledge worker.

The rise of the knowledge worker is a trend that is as irresistible and as profound as the move from mainframes to PCs, and the impact of mobile and the internet on the way we live and work. The race is on to provide knowledge workers with the tools and virtual assistants that will enable them to do a lot of the work today that historically has been done by 'professionals', whether they are IT developers, lawyers, HR advisers, etc. We are witnessing the flattening of organisations and the empowering of knowledge workers. We will also see tools put in the hands of customers (whether individuals or businesses) that traditionally were used by professional intermediaries, whether in medical, financial, legal, or other areas.

In the very near future, knowledge workers in any function who are the subject matter experts and who are closest to the customer and/or business need, will be able to undertake activities that previously required IT departments, change control, IT developers, and software houses; changes that took significant time and cost to deliver. We all have war stories about the difficulty and frustrations of trying to change enterprise-wide platforms for even the simplest purposes!

Using a legal example as a proxy, imagine that a knowledge worker in a legal team whose only IT expertise is their ability to use Microsoft Office can quickly build, maintain, and evolve an end-to-end customer, local, or complex global workflow and process including:

1. Instruction management (what legal support, if any, does the individual/ business unit actually need?);
2. Triage (if legal support is required, who should it be undertaken by, internally or externally, given the requirement and its risk, time, cost profile?);
3. Case management and document creation (how can the matter be managed consistently, using the right documents and with the appropriate data captured consistently, whoever is doing the work?); and
4. Reporting and analytics (how is real-time activity published so resource can be managed, and how are trends and data mining undertaken to pre-empt future risk, reduce cost, and evolve the operating model?)

This redefines the traditional IT and business operating model. It changes the way legal and other functions operate. This model is available today. We already operate this way in Riverview Law by deploying easy-to-use expert systems, automation, artificial intelligence, and analytics. Internally, we call this the 'configuration, not coding' revolution: using knowledge workers with easy-to-use configuration tools to manage day-to-day requirements, rather than IT developers with programming skills. Yes, we still need IT programmers. Yes, we still need lawyers and other professionals. But their focus changes. IT programmers help build the tools and platforms that unleash knowledge workers and the business. Lawyers start to play the real added-value parts in the legal process.

This approach also helps us and our customers to address the absolutely critical need for accurate data. In the 'big (medium or small) data' debate, if data (content) is king, the ability to properly understand and apply it (context) is the kingdom. Of course, the keys to the kingdom include capturing the data accurately, consistently, and easily in real time. Which neatly brings us all the way back to workflows and processes, which need to be automated and amended easily, quickly, and cost-effectively by knowledge workers so that they reflect business needs.

The big disconnect

This all partly explains the challenges we sometimes experience at Riverview Law as we engage with the legal industry. With notable exceptions, in particular our conversations with in-house teams and a few legal leaders who 'get it', it has felt as though two conversations have been occurring in parallel.

On one side are the current legal players (Law 1.0) with their pre-occupation with PEP, lateral hires, international expansion, mergers, and (particularly in the US) maintaining the regulatory status quo. Their focus is on using IT to improve their current operating and business model. Their pre-occupation is with Law 1.0 and a desire, on the part of many, to delay Law 2.0.

On the other side are the new entrants, including technology companies and businesses like Riverview Law (and some in-house teams), who have brought disciplines, business models, and technology from other sectors. These players are focused not just on creating a profitable Law 2.0 platform, but also on using this platform to transition quickly to Law 3.0. They – we – use the language of the customer, the culture of one team, and the application of existing and emerging technologies, including automation, analytics, and computational argumentation, to drive quality and improve efficiency.

The new legal giants

Of course, for legal there is a big irony in all this. Over many decades, the legal market has not been subjected to the same competitive pressures that other sectors of the economy have experienced. Whatever lawyers and law firms may think, they have benefitted from protective regulations that enabled excess profits. This, inevitably, injected complacency in many of its incumbents and reduced innovation and creativity. The irony is that the very regulation that protected Law 1.0 firms has also sown the seeds for their substitution as Law 2.0 and, more critically, Law 3.0 models take over. It would be difficult for many law firms to respond to the emerging competition in the legal vertical in any event, but when this is combined with technology upheaval, all bets are off.

This does not mean that there aren't great opportunities, because there are. It also doesn't mean that some Law 1.0 players won't successfully transition to Law 2.0 and Law 3.0, because some will. The legal market is a global market and, as with all markets, there is no silver bullet and there is no one-size-fits-all model that will succeed.

Moreover, in England and Wales, we have been dealt a good hand by our legislators and regulators. If we can combine the best of our regulatory model with the best of existing and emerging technologies, particularly those coming out of the US, then we are in a good position to dominate the global legal market in the first half of this century. By focusing on Law 3.0 and working with Silicon Valley, we can become the new legal giants. What a great time to be a technology-led legal services business.

About the author

Karl Chapman is chief executive of Riverview Law and has a long pedigree in starting, growing, and managing successful companies.

After reading law at Birmingham University, Karl joined Guinness Mahon Investment Management (GMIM) in 1985. In 1987, he was Money Observer's top-performing UK unit trust fund manager. He left GMIM in 1989 to set up CRT Group plc (CRT), a consultancy, recruitment, and training business. Under Karl's leadership, his team grew CRT, both organically and by acquisition, to a market capitalisation of over £600 million, sales in excess of £400 million, with 2,500 employees operating from over 200 locations. In 1996, CRT sold 50.1 percent of its equity for £109 million to Knowledge Universe, a private US-based company whose major shareholders were Larry Ellison and Michael Milken. Karl left CRT in 2000 and set up AdviserPlus Business Solutions in 2001. AdviserPlus is a leading advisory outsourcing organisation providing HR and H&S solutions to organisations, ranging from FTSE 100 companies to SMEs. He joined Riverview Law with effect from 1 June 2011.

Karl is excited by the changes taking place in the legal market: 'Rarely do market opportunities like this arise. The legal market is large, fragmented, and has few brands. New entrants like Riverview Law, with no baggage and a total focus on the customer, stand a very good chance of building big and sustainable businesses.'

Karl is based in London and Lincolnshire and couples his passion for business with a long-standing love of Chelsea Football Club where, over more than 40 years, he has experienced the lows and highs that come with an irrational attachment to a football team.

www.ingramcontent.com/pod-product-compliance
Ingram Content Group UK Ltd.
Pitfield, Milton Keynes, MK11 3LW, UK
UKHW050231160926
8657IPUK00008B/195